Joining the Army &

Surviving and Completing Basic Combat Training

Forward

When I decided to join the milit what I was getting myself into or what I would be doing once I arrived at basic training. I did some research on-line and managed to find a few things like people talking about how bored they were during reception or what they were going to do with their enlistment bonus but nothing that told me what I could expect. I also found some short videos showing me the gas chamber and a leadership reaction course but again, nothing that could really prepare me for what was coming. I was getting more and more nervous as my ship out date drew closer and I found myself asking people who had previously served in the Army what they remembered about basic training. Sadly, the only thing they could offer was that it was a long time ago.

After arriving at basic training, I was astounded at how much there was to learn and even more shocked that no one was willing to talk about any of it! Then, about four weeks into my training, I sustained an injury that would prevent me from graduating that cycle however, it wouldn't prevent me from graduating eventually. Although I wasn't allowed to participate in all of the training exercises I was still given all of the training and I stayed with my company until they graduated.

While I was recovering from my injury though, I thought to myself, 'I should write a book about basic training that would help future soldiers in preparing for their time here.' I had already been taking notes as I progressed though the training, but now I started writing down everything in a way that would allow me to write this book once I completed my training and graduated. Once I received the medical care I needed, I started over as a day one restart with the same battalion but a new company.

Your ten weeks at basic training are not that difficult **if you are properly prepared for it**. My first cycle was a little rough and stressful only because I didn't know what to expect. My second cycle was a lot easier because I knew what to expect and when we had 'free time' I was sharing my first cycle notes with my platoon which helped everyone to prepare for what was coming.

Before you dive into my book I want you to know a few things and the first thing you should know is that your basic training will not be like mine. Every cycle is different, drill sergeants learn and evolve into better instructors, they change things up in a way that will best benefit their platoon. You will be learning everything that I learned but the things you learn may have newer procedures or you may have newer equipment than what I was trained with. With that being said, I won't be teaching you how to do everything but I will be informing you of the things I went through, what I learned and what you'll be expected to learn. You will also do some of the things in my book in a different order, I for example did map reading and land navigation in red phase with my first cycle and in my second cycle we did it at the end of white phase. This is due to the fact that your company will have to reserve specific areas for your training and there are other companies trying to reserve those same areas too.

I went to Fort Benning, GA and was with Battalion 2/47 where our battalion motto was 'Panthers Never Quit'. I started out in Bravo Company and after 6 months I finished with Foxtrot Company. Battalion 2/47 was the hardest in Fort Benning for non-infantry (or so I was told), and Bravo company was definitely the hardest company in that battalion during my time there. I went through two cycles with two different companies and I got to spend time with every company in that battalion. Because of all those experiences, I will be taking the best of what everyone had to teach me and will use them as a template to prepare you for your training. Also, I was not infantry and even though everyone goes though the same basic training, infantry will have an additional two phases that my book will not cover.

Your Recruiter

When most people think about joining the military the first thought that pops into their head is picking a branch, speaking to a recruiter and then getting on a bus to go to their basic training. Unfortunately, it's a little more involved than that.

Selecting a branch and speaking with a recruiter is easy and if you want to be lazy about it, you just show up and do what they tell you. If, however, you want to be smart about it you won't limit yourself to looking at just one branch and visiting that one recruiter. This is a critical point in your military career and if you don't do a little bit of legwork it's going to come back to haunt you later. Speak to a recruiter from each branch of the military, this will give you a feel for what each branch of the service is like and will allow you to see all of your options, if you let your recruiters know that you're exploring other branches they're going to put in that extra effort to get you into their branch.

A recruiter will sell you which ever branch of the military your recruiter is recruiting for and they are very good at it. Before you visit a recruiter though, make a list of things you would like to get out of the military such as; are you looking for the benefits? Travel? How physically demanding is this branch? Will they pay for college? What Military Occupational Specialty (MOS) are available to me? Try and make it a hard sale for the recruiter, negotiate the best deal you can. By speaking with a recruiter from each branch you may find that one branch has a lot more to offer you than the branch you were originally drawn to.

Call your recruiters as much as you like, this is your future and they are there to answer your questions. Do not be afraid to call your recruiter 20, 50 or even 100 times, they will work with you and remember, only 1% of the United States population joins the military, **they want you**! This is a volunteer army, so when you go in and see a

4

recruiter, you're not being interviewed for a job, you're interviewing them and seeing if you want this job. After you have a clear picture of what each branch has to offer, make your choice and proceed with the one that benefits you the most. Remember, you are under no obligation to do anything because you've spoken with a recruiter one or one hundred times.

If you're looking at the Army be sure to ask if they have a copy of the soldier's blue book and make sure to take pamphlets and anything else the recruiters will give you. Try setting up your ideal job in the military, write everything down and when you visit your recruiters to see if they can fit you into this ideal job or close to it. Know too, that there will be more MOS's available to choose from if you go active military than there are if you go to the Reserves or the National Guard.

Once you have decided on what branch you want, you will be asked to provide specific documents such as birth certificates, marriage certificates, education records and other things that they will need in order to get you into the system. If you have any college be sure and mention that because that can count towards obtaining a higher rank in the military which means more pay. I already had by bachelor's degree when I joined and so I started out as an E-4 (Specialist) when I went to basic training.

MEPS

Military Entrance Processing Station (MEPS) is your next step in joining the military once you've selected a branch. You will be given a date to report to a hotel where you will stay the night before going to MEPS. Your recruiter will give you a packet, which you will need to bring to MEPS along with a photo I.D. When you arrive at the hotel you will go up to the counter and tell them you are there for MEPS. They will ask you for a photo I.D. and mark you down on a list. You will then be told the rules of the hotel, the wing you stay in may be specially reserved for MEPS purposes. You will then you will be shown to your room and you be given a meal voucher which will allow you to get dinner in the hotel or elsewhere if the hotel doesn't offer dinner services.

You will be woken up early in the morning to go to MEPS. Collect all of your things from you room because you probably won't be going back. (Sometimes MEPS can take up to several days and you will return to the hotel, but you may not be in the same room. Be sure to take all of your belongings with you unless otherwise instructed.) Once you've eaten your breakfast you will be lined up and put on a bus that will take you to the MEPS building. You will then be put into a formation and lined up outside the MEPS building where you will wait to be enter the building, have your photo I.D. ready because they will check it before putting you through a metal detector and having your bags x-rayed.

Once you have passed through security you will place your belongings in a cabinet (your phone must be stored with your belongings) and report to the branch office of the military you have chosen to go with. Once you are at your branch office, they will mark you down on their files as having made it there, give you a packet and tell you where to go to continue your processing. Your next stop will probably have you sitting in a waiting room for a time. You will check in at the counter by showing them a photo I.D., give them your full social security number and an electronic fingerprint will be taken.

Your next stop will be sitting in a room where you will be briefed about paperwork concerning prior medical conditions, allergies and so forth. You will sign a document stating you have provided all the necessary information fully and truthfully. They will then explain the different stations you will be going to and what will happen if you don't finish today.

MEPS is where you will be examined to ensure you meet all of the physical requirements to join the military. The things you can expect to be done here are: You will have your blood drawn, do a urine analysis, eye test, hearing test, a physical, height and weight and speak with a doctor a few times. You will have to take an ASVAB test during or before you arrive at MEPS, this will show them what you're most qualified to do and will determine what MOS you're qualified for. If you don't qualify for what you want, don't be afraid to study and retake the ASVAB to try and get what you want. I recommend looking up the ASVAB test and studying, the better you do on this test, the better your choices will be for what MOS you will be able to choose from.

Once you have finished testing, you'll then return to your branch office inside of MEPS (The office you first checked into) and they will give you some more paperwork to fill out before going through a list of available MOS's for you to choose from. After selecting your MOS they will select when and where you will start your basic training. If you need more time before starting for any reason (e.g. need to get finances in order, want to give your notice at work, want to spend time with family or you need to get into shape) ask them for a later start date, they will agree and let you start later.

After you have completed all of the tests and have chosen your MOS, you will be taken to another area where you will read over a contract and prepare to sign it but before you do, you will be taken into a room with others and you will be sworn in. Once you have finished swearing in you will return to your contract and sign it. *Congratulations*, you are now in the military. You will then be taken back to the hotel and may return home from there.

My MEPS experience was very good and although it lasted most of the day I can say I was happy with how it turned out. I have heard horror stories about MEPS too, mostly about it taking several days to get through. Prepare for the worst and hope for the best. Also, if by any chance you're unfortunate enough to have a bad experience in store for you there, take something to read to help pass the time, take this book and see what else is in store for you!

Before Basic

For many of you this could be the most important section in the entire book because this is going to help prepare you physically and mentally for basic training. A common mistake people make is waiting until they arrive at basic training to get into shape. The reason this is a mistake is because once you arrive at basic you don't want the pressure of having to get into shape while learning everything they will be throwing at you. Basic training is exhausting both physically and mentally so the less you have to do once you arrive, the less stress you'll have to endure. Also, when you're at basic training, you will be doing workouts on their schedule and there won't be much time to do anything additional work outs. It's so much easier for you to start working out now, doing what you can and taking a break when you need one. You don't have to kill yourself with working out right now, simply doing workouts and getting into the habit of doing them correctly will make a big difference later on.

In basic training you will be getting up at 0400 or close to it so it doesn't hurt to start working on getting up earlier and going to bed earlier. A piece of advice given to me from a wounded trainee at basic training was to run everywhere you go and you will get into shape or stay in shape better that way. I'm not talking running to the store from your house, although you could, but if you're going to the store, park on the far side of the parking lot, jog to the store from there, or if you are going over to your neighbor's house jog over there.

Another thing you're going to want to start doing is cutting back on your junk food, fast food, all Tabaco products and start taking multivitamins, getting plenty of calcium and potassium in your system. If you wait until basic to cut these habits you may find it's a lot harder than you thought but some people in basic stopped smoking the day they arrived and were fine so this is your choice, you know your mental strength and limitations best.

Stretches: Stretching is very important, you'll be using your muscles in ways you're not use to and your body needs to remain flexible while doing this. Doing good stretches will prevent injuries from occurring while you're doing workouts. Look up stretches that work your hips, legs and arms. Proper stretching will also aid you if you have a pulled muscle or other types of pain. If a certain stretch helps you before a run, get into the habit of doing that stretch when you wake up before morning P.T.

Push-ups: Do push-ups, this is the best way you can prepare yourself for doing them. Find a good hand position when you're doing your push-ups and just start knocking them out, if that means you can only do five then do sets of five. The most important thing to remember is making sure you do them correctly, meaning going all the way down until your chest nearly hits the ground or your triceps are parallel to the ground. There are different types of push-ups you can do too, there are wide arm push-ups where you place your hands further apart than a normal push-up, normal push-ups where your hands are directly under you, and diamond push-ups, where your hands are together making a diamond shape with your thumbs and pointing fingers touching.

When doing the Army Physical Fitness Test (APFT) any of these push-ups are allowed and you can move your hands just as long as they never leave the mat surface. Remember to do them correctly! It doesn't matter if you can knock out 200 bad push-ups in two minutes because they won't count, you want whatever drill sergeant is grading you to count every one of your push-ups. There are other exercises you can do as well to build up your arms and chest but the best way to prepare for doing push-ups is to do push-ups.

Sit-ups: Do Sit-ups and other core exercises. One of my drill sergeants had us perform a workout with him that was an ab killer and I'm going to share it with you:

10-15 crunches (holding for two seconds your elbow to your knee)

10-15 oblique's (this is like a crunch but you're taking your right elbow to your left knee, and then your left elbow to your right knee, holding for two seconds)

20 straight crunches

4 count Flutter kicks X 50 (Placing your hands just under your bottom, raise your feet about 10 inches above the ground and start kicking back and forth, each time your

right leg makes a full motion up and down you've done one.) So for this exercise you are doing four counts for one set and you are doing 50 sets without stopping.

20 Leg spreads (Raise your feet 6 inches above the ground and simply open them for 2 seconds and close them.

Leg raises (Raise your feet 2 inches above the ground and raise them all the way up and back down to two inches above the ground, do this until you cannot do any more, this is called burnout.)

Roll over to your stomach like you are going to do a pushup and push your stomach down toward the ground while holding yourself up with your arms, this should stretch your stomach muscles.

Repeat these exercises 3 times. You do not take a break between the exercises and only a short break between sets. Remember, you are doing this to get ready for basic training, if you cheat this exercise you're only cheating yourself.

Running: Run as far/ long as you can without stopping. Find a comfortable pace to run at and time yourself for a 2-mile run, this will show you where you're at and how much better you need to be. It's alright if you can't run two miles straight without stopping, you're going to build up to it, just keep running and pushing yourself to run as far as you can with as little break as possible. Your run doesn't have to be very fast, just work on building up your endurance for now and worry about time later.

When I started I couldn't run one mile without several stops for air, and then one day I said I was going to start running two miles and pushed myself for a second mile. I took a lot more breaks but I made sure that I was running most of it and I would run it twice a day (except weekends) and it wasn't that long before I was building up the endurance I would need to complete the run. Don't think you have to be able to run it all at once when you start, that's why you're doing this training now so that when the military makes you run those long distances you'll be prepared for it.

You can also build up leg strength by doing lunges, squats and running up and down stairs. Stair running really helped a number of our guys in basic training to improve their run time so if you have stairs or a stair climber you can do this along with your running.

Rucking: In the Army you will be going out on ruck marches A ruck march is where you're wearing your army uniform, an assault bag or a ruck sack filled with gear and you will be marching 2, 4, 8, 10 and 16 KM. I recommend you throw on some boots, a backpack filled with 20- 40 LB in your bag and start marching to build up your leg strength. This can also be rough on your bones, so if you're not use to this type of thing, you'll want calcium in your diet in order to strengthen your bones up so you don't get stress fractures. (Stress fracture are not that uncommon in basic training and they can be very annoying so it's better to work on strengthening your bones now.)

There's more to the military than just working out though, if you want to get ahead of the game you're going to want to start studying the following things I've listed here:

The Soldiers Creed

I am an American Soldier

I am a warrior and a member of a team

I serve the people of the United States and live the army values

I will always place the mission first

I will never accept defeat

I will never quit

I will never leave a fallen comrade

I am disciplined, physically and mentally tough, trained and proficient in my warrior tasks and drills

I always maintain my arms, my equipment and myself

I am an expert and a professional

I stand ready to deploy, engage and destroy the enemies of the United States of America in close combat

I am a guardian of freedom and the American way of life

I am an American soldier

Warriors Ethos

The Warriors Ethos is in the Soldiers creed, I put it in a bold font and underlined it.

General Orders

1. I will guard everything within the limits of my post and quit my post only when properly relieved.
2. I will obey my special orders and perform all of my duties in a military manner.
3. I will report violations of my special orders, emergencies and anything not covered in my instructions to the commander of the relief.

Army Values: L.D.R.S.H.I.P.

Loyalty. Duty. Respect. Selfless Service. Honor. Integrity. Personal Courage

The Army Song

March along, sing our song, with the Army of the free
Count the brave, count the true, who have fought to victory
We're the Army and proud of our name
We're the Army and proudly proclaim

First to fight for the right,
And to build the nation's might,
And the Army goes rolling along
Proud of all we have done,
Fighting till the battle's won,
And the Army goes rolling along.

Then it's Hi! Hi! Hey!
The Army's on its way.
Count off the cadence loud and strong
For where e'er we go,
You will always know
That The Army Goes Rolling Along.

You will also need to know the chain of command, start with the President of the United States, Secretary of Defense, Secretary of the Army and the Chief of Staff and so on going down the line. You will also need to know your chain of command for your company but you won't see that until you arrive at your company in basic training.

Memorize these things so that you can recite them in front of a crowd of people word for word. You will be tested on this in basic training as well so it's good to learn them now while you have the time. When my first platoon was ready to graduate I had several people come over to me and tell me that they were able to remember me from reception because when asked to recite the soldier's creed in front of everyone perfectly, I was the only one able to do it. Because of that a lot of people had a lot of respect for me though I never knew it until they told me so before they left for A.I.T. I had the drill sergeant even come up to me after words and tell me that not many people can stand up in front of people and recite the soldier's creed perfectly in reception. Many people will know the creed in reception but they'll choke or hesitate at points when trying to say in in front of others because they haven't rehearsed it enough to be confident in reciting it in front of others.

Leaving Home

Your recruiter should give you a list of things you will need at basic training but you won't need to actually bring much with you. Most of what you'll need you'll be getting once you get to reception. Pack very light, you should only need one or two sets of clothing and maybe some personal pictures of family, and an address book. (You may want to bring zip lock bags along because you can store your notes and your blue book in them making them water proof in case you should you get caught in the rain or fall into a body of water.) Avoid bringing any over the counter drugs (prescription is fine as long as they know about it and you must have the prescription). Things like porn, food, drinks, weapons, Tabaco, weapons and anything valuable that you don't want to lose, you should leave at home. Take your cell phone and a charger if you have one, you will have a few chances to make phone calls in basic training, if you don't have one though you could ask to borrow someone else's.

The day before you ship out to basic training you will return to the hotel you stayed at for MEPS. The following morning you will return to MEPS to receive instructions and a packet with information that you will be handing over to someone once you arrive at reception. <u>Do not open or loose this packet!</u> You will also receive meal vouchers and an explanation on how and where to use them. If you don't use the meal vouchers you have to turn them in once you arrive at reception and since these will be your last good meals until training is over, I recommend you take advantage of them. They will then bus you to the airport and you will be on your way.

You will most likely have a direct flight to where ever you are going so you only need to worry about where to meet up once you arrive. One or more sergeants will come to pick you up at the airport. They'll have you get into a formation, place your bags at your feet and show them the packet you received at MEPS. You will then be marched down the halls into a room where you will sign in before being put on a bus and taken to reception. The ride may take a while so this would be a good time to use your cell phone to make some last-minute phone calls to your friends and loved ones.

<u>Reception</u>

When you arrive at reception you will be given a warm, motivating welcoming speech. After you've been welcomed you will be taught how to stand at attention, stand at ease and then filed into the reception building. Once inside, there will be some wooden benches or seats where you will be seated and wait for a drill sergeant to come in and give you a briefing about contraband. Contraband is anything not allowed such as: weapons, drugs, food, porn, gambling items and pretty much anything aside from the clothes on your back and anything you were ordered to bring.

After the contraband briefing is over you will be taken to an amnesty room where you will be allowed to dispose of all of your contraband items. If you have any contraband this is your chance to get rid of it because once you leave this room, any contraband found on you can result in disciplinary actions. Do not put your cell phone, your wallet or anything you want to keep into the amnesty slots, this is only for stuff that you are throwing away and with that said, don't ask if you can get any of it back after training, you have thrown it away, it's gone.

Now you will receive a copy of the Soldiers Blue Book and an advanced tactics book. The blue book contains useful information about the different phases you will be going through, the soldier's creed, the Army song, regulations about your uniform, Sexual Harassment Assault Response & Prevention (S.H.A.R.P.) as well as other important information that you will use throughout basic training.

After you have been briefed again about contraband, (They want to make sure you know what it is and that you shouldn't ever have it), you will be marched down to another room where you will be given paperwork to fill out. Once the paperwork is done, some civilians will begin to issue you your physical training (P.T.) clothing and a duffel bag. Most of your gear will be issued to you by civilians, be polite and respectful to them.

After you've gone through all the lectures you'll collect your things and march over to the barracks that you'll be staying at while in reception. Once you're at the barracks you be put into a formation that has you two arm lengths away from the person on your left and right. You will then be instructed to empty your personal bag out and you will be told the things you may keep out (e.g. your wallet and paperwork) and put them into your new duffle bag. Everything else, including your cell phones will be placed in your personal bag. They will do a check to ensure you have everything that was just issued to you and that you have all of the paperwork that you will need.

You will then be told to go inside and change into your P.T. uniform. You will also take this time to fill up your camel back with water before returning to your formation. Once you are back in formation you will place your civilian clothes in your personal bag and zip it up. A Sergeant will then show you to a room inside the barracks where you will place your civilian bag, it will be locked up for the duration of reception. You will take your duffle bag and be shown to your room and be assigned a bunk.

The next day you will be given an advance in pay in the amount of $250.00 on an Eagle Cash Card, which works like a gift card (anyone can use it if you lose it so don't lose it). You will have no need for cash or any other form of money until you are finished with basic training unless you lose articles of clothing and need to replace them, which can get expensive so try not to lose anything. There also may come a time when you can buy other things and you will need money, but that will be for novelty items or food. Right after you receive your Eagle Cash Card you will then be taken to get a haircut, you can ask for any type of haircut you like but it's all getting shaved off, you will all have the exact same haircut. (If you're a female you get to keep a little.)

This being your first full night in reception you will have a chance to experience fireguard or staff duty. Fireguard will consist of you and a battle buddy walking around your sleeping quarters ensuring that everyone is in their beds and that everyone in the room belongs there. If someone is in your room that is suicidal you will also be watching him or her to ensure they do not try and commit suicide, this is called suicide watch. You will also take a head count of everyone in their beds and report it to the staff duty. Another group of two of you will be posted at the staff duty desk next to a sergeant where you will write down everything that goes on during the night, including the counts from each of the sleeping quarters. Each shift is one hour long before you're relieved by the next group.

The next day you will be gathered in an auditorium where you will be filling out paperwork, mostly you'll be putting your name on a couple of things and verifying many other things. A sergeant will then ask everyone if there's anything they're allergic to or conditions they need to report that are not in their files. At this point you will truly learn the meaning of the term 'Hurry up and wait'. You will begin getting your shots, one of which will be a penicillin shot in the butt followed by a few other minor shots and then you will have your blood drawn. (I myself hate getting shots and I am very bad about getting my blood drawn, the people have giving them are very good, I barely felt a thing during any of it.) After getting your penicillin shot you will want to massage the area from time to time good and hard so it will spread throughout your body, otherwise it can become hard and then you will have to have it removed and receive another penicillin shot. (At least that's what they tell us when we're there.)

Once you have finished with the shots you will be marched down to the PX where you will purchase some necessary items such as hygiene products, flashlights and new running shoes. Make sure that the shoes are very comfortable, don't be afraid to tell them if they are uncomfortable because you will be spending a lot of money on them and doing PT in them for quite a while. Be sure to purchase stamps, envelops and a couple good pens for writing your letters. You will have an option to buy an army watch there as well, I recommend buying the watch before you leave home because the watch they sale is pretty expensive and doesn't do anything more than tell time, set an alarm and contain a stopwatch. Also, the drill sergeants may have you remove your watches for a majority of basic training, in both of my cycles we were told to remove our watches and were only allowed to start using them during land navigation.

The next day you will be doing a physical assessment consisting of one pull-up and a one-mile run. This assessment is used to determine where you stand physically. Once you've completed the assessment you will be marched over to where you received your P.T. uniform and you will receive your main uniform. You will be filed through a line where someone will look at you and decide what size you are and hand you a piece of your uniform. This will be done for each piece and you will receive four uniforms in total. You will also receive socks, pants, shirts, jackets, underwear, two protective covers (P.C.) which is your hat, and a belt. Putting on the uniform for the first time will fill you with pride, you'll be able to look in the mirror and see a reflection of the man or woman you are going to be.

From here you will be taken to another section of the building where you will fill out more paperwork ranging from insurance to marriage and dependents. You will want to have the copies of your paperwork such as your birth certificate, marriage certificate and any other important documents you brought with you, I recommend having at least six and don't give your last one away, you may need it. You will also fill out paperwork regarding your common access card (CAC) which is your military I.D. Do not lose this I.D. because it is a sensitive item that contains a lot of your information. Also, this is an inspectable item so always have it on you. The only time you will be allowed to not have it with you is during physical training (P.T.) and that is only because it's easy to lose in your P.T. uniform. You will receive a password sometime in the future, possibly in white phase or blue phase to access your CAC and you will use this to access specific sites on-line to verify information or to fill out surveys.

The next day you will stand or sit in a line and wait to be fitted to your new boots. Whatever size shoe you wear now, don't expect it in these boots, they will measure your foot, they will place a pair of boots in front of you, you will then put one boot on and walk around a little in it. It's important you tell them if it's comfortable or not, if it feels tight then tell them because these are going to be the boots you wear for at least ten weeks or longer. If one of your feet is bigger than the other, try the boot on that foot when you walk around testing it out. You will receive three pairs of boots all together, two normal pair that you will wear every day and one cold weather pair of boots that you probably won't have any use for while you are in basic training unless you're there in the winter months. Try and get a good feel for your boots over the next few days, you will break your boots in a little and if your feet start hurting to much or they start bleeding in those few days, let your sergeant know and they will try and get you back to get new boots.

When you find time, go ahead and mark your boots and your shoes. I took a Sharpe and wrote my name on the inside part of the tongue. You will do this because when your sleeping quarters gets flipped, and they all get flipped and torn apart, your shoes and boots may get tossed around the room and it's easier to get yours back if they're marked. You may also want to tie a knot at the end of your boot laces so when you're getting out of your boots, you don't pull the laces out.

You'll now start going through different stations for evaluations. One station will test your eye sight, another will take x-rays of your teeth and make a mouth guard for you and another station will test your hearing. If you need glasses or contacts be sure and bring them with you because they will be making you a pair of army glasses which are supposed to be nearly indestructible, and they will make you prescription inserts for your eye pro. This will take the better part of the day and you will be going in to each station in small groups.

The next day you'll get to look forward to getting more shots and being issued your hearing protection. You'll take a class on how to use your hearing protection properly along with how hearing damage can be permanent if you don't take care of your ears. This should be one of the last days you'll be at reception, at least it will be one of the last days you'll need to do anything at reception.

You probably won't believe this right now but reception is often times considered the worst part of getting through basic training because of all the time you spend doing nothing. Whenever you're not standing in line or doing paperwork, you will be sitting in a chair or a hard bench reading your soldiers blue book, this is a good time to review the soldier's creed, the 3 general orders and the army song though. Try to memorize all of these so that you can recite them perfectly in front of a crowd, the sergeants there may test you from time to time by having you recite one of these in front of everyone.

Enjoy your meals in reception, they are fairly relaxed, you will also have a choice as to what you eat and there will even be something resembling snacks like pudding and cake. You won't be getting these opportunities once you get to your training unit.

On your final night in reception you will pack all of your things into the two duffle bags that you have, this will be a seemingly impossible task, the first of many you will face. First thing you will want to do is to ranger roll all of your clothes, you will also want to stuff as many of your clothes into your boots and shoes as you possibly can. You will be stuffing everything so tight that it will barely close but it is possible. You will then take all of your stuff, including your personal bag, outside where you will leave it.

Two of you will be posted as guards to watch over all of the bags in addition to the staff duty and fireguards. The next morning you may or may not be able to get breakfast at reception, if you do get to eat breakfast, right after you will sit on your bags until the busses come to take you to your training unit Once the busses arrive you will have the pleasure of meeting your drill sergeants for the first time. These drill sergeants will tell you to place one duffle bag on your back, one on your front and to carry your personal bag in your hands and load up onto a bus. Once everyone is on the bus a drill sergeant will load up with you and you will be taken 'down range' to your new barracks. Down range is a term the drill sergeants will use to refer to your training area and you will only hear it referred to like this while you are in reception and only the drill sergeants will be using this term, once you are in your training area the term will typically refer to the shooting range. On the way down, you will be given brief instructions by the drill sergeant about what he expects of you and what you will do once you get there.

One final note about reception, the drill sergeants may or may not be allowed to punish you with physical exercise. When and where I went they were not allowed to punish you with physical exercises while I was in reception. Other training sites though have different rules and they may be allowed to punish you in such a way.

Destination - Basic Combat Training

Now you're ready to start your ten-week training routine, sorry but the week you just spent in reception doesn't count as training but you will still get paid for it. Basic training consists of three stages, also called phases and they are red, white and blue. Each phase has a test at the end that must be passed in order to progress to the next phase. You will start out in 'Red Phase' which tells everyone that you are at the very beginning of your training. Red phase is by far the hardest phase to get through because you have so much to learn in a short amount of time and you have to prove yourself worthy of the added benefits that come with the other phases. The most noticeable benefit I noticed when we got to white and eventually blue phase was that we were allowed to march ourselves over to the mess hall when it was time for chow, or we could go to sick call in battle buddy teams instead of being escorted there by a sergeant. Any time spent away from drill sergeants is good. Other benefits you won't notice quite so much but they are there just the same are things like you will get punished less. The drill sergeants may start telling you entertaining and personal stories of their time in the military and become a little less hostile. Instead of getting smoked for doing something stupid, you'll be cleaning your weapons or studying for an upcoming test.

Each platoon has a phase banner and on it will be a colored flag indicating what phase your platoon is currently in. Even though the entire company should be in the same phase at all times, if a platoon is doing stupid stuff or isn't performing up to standards, a platoon can be demoted to a previous phase having their benefits taken away. For the duration of this book I will list things you will likely be learning in each phase, keep in mind that sometimes something I have listed in one phase, could actually be taught in another phase, for example, in my first cycle we were taught land navigation from the beginning of red phase, however in my second cycle we didn't get to land navigation until near the end of white phase.

Shark Attack

As soon as the bus pulls up to your barracks you should see several drill sergeants waiting for you and as soon as the bus doors open they will be yelling at you to get off of the bus. Move as quickly as you can and try not to get stopped by a drill sergeant, the best thing to do is follow everyone else and not stop for anything, if you happen to be the first one off the bus just head in the direction the drill sergeants are pointing, you'll figure out where to go. Once you are where you are supposed to be the drill sergeants will have you get into some type of formation and a favorite thing of theirs to do is to have you hold all of your bags above your head and not lower them until they say. Drill sergeants will take this opportunity to start yelling at you and everyone else.

You may do this or maybe you'll be doing some sitting down and then standing up with your bags or running up and down stairs with your bags. Whatever the drill sergeants find entertaining to have you do, it's just there way of breaking you in. Once they've tired of this they will have you spread out and they'll do an inventory of all of your things. First, they'll have you dump everything out of your duffels. They will then go through a list of things you were recently issued and you will have to hold them up showing them that you have them. (This was the check list they used for me in basic training.)

- Army Uniform Top   4
- Army Uniform Trousers   4
- Patrol Cap   2
- Hot weather boots   2 pair
- Cold weather boots   1 pair
- Tan T-shirt   7
- Green Socks   7 pair
- Tan underwear   7
- Fleece PT cap   1
- Black P.T. jacket   1
- P.T. Pants   1
- P.T. Shorts   3
- P.T. Short Sleeve T-shirt   3
- P.T. Long Sleeve T-shirt   2
- White Socks   7 pair
- P.T. Shoes   1 pair
- Brown Towel   4
- Brown Wash Cloth   4
- Black dress socks   7 pair
- Waffle Top   1
- Waffle Bottom   1
- Silk Top   1
- Silk Bottom   1
- Fleece Gray Top   1
- Wet Weather Top   1
- Eye Protection   1
- Leather Gloves   1 pair
- Glove Inserts   1 pair
- Laundry Bag   1

- Knee & Elbow inserts   4 total
- Flashlight (with batteries)   1
- Padlock with keys   1
- Shower Shoes   1 pair
- Tooth Brush Case   1
- Soap Case   1
- Razors
- Shaving cream
- Profiles and Medicine
- Paperwork, Bible, Wallet, I.D. Card, Debit Card, Eagle Cash Card, Stationary, Watch.

Once they've gone through everything they will tell you what is not allowed and may have you throw things away like liquid soap, laundry soap pods and whatever this particular group has decided you are not allowed to have. You will then be told to take out the eye pro you received and attach the clear lenses. Your company may or may not require you to wear them at all times, just don't lose them because it can cost about $70.00 to replace.

Once you've done a complete inventory you will stuff everything back into your duffels and set them aside. You will then be instructed to take your personal bag and place it into a locked room, make sure your cell phone, cell phone charger, wallet and anything you may need is not in this bag! You will not see it again until basic training is over and if you forget something inside of it the drill sergeants will not be happy with you and may require you to do some 'Volunteer P.T.' for not grabbing it in the first place. The only things in your personal bag should be things like your MP3 player, head phones, fun books, cards, anything else you brought for entertainment and your civilian clothing.

At this time, you will probably be given a roster number, this number will be your new identification and will be used as often, if not more often, than your name while in training. This number will identify which platoon you are in and which person in that platoon you are, for example if you are 237, then you belong to second platoon, you're the 37th person issued to that platoon. If you are 460, you belong to 4th platoon and are the 60th person in that platoon. Each platoon can have up to 60 people and you are usually numbered alphabetically by last name. You will then be sent up to your bay where you will find your bunk, each bunk is numbered and you will have a locker assigned to you as well.

Inventory

Now you've just finished making sure that you have all of the gear that was issued to you and you're eager to place it into your locker but when you open your locker you'll find that it's already filled with more gear including a duffle bag containing even more gear! You will be instructed to pull the duffle bag out along with all of the additional gear in your locker and toe the line with it. The drill sergeant will then do an inventory of the gear. Some of the gear you will find inside is; a sleeping mat, a whoopee, army combat helmet (ACH), ACH cover, wet weather bag, assault bag (military back pack that you will take with you when you go out to ranges or courses), improved first aid kit (IFAK), a canteen, canteen holder, flick (looks like a vest) two sleeping bags and sleeping bag holders, tent stakes (you probably won't get a tent though), grenade pouch, magazine pouches, sling, knee pads and elbow pads. Your locker may also have some sunscreen, a blank firing adapter (BFA) foot powder, instruction booklets and or miscellaneous other things or that may be kept in an area where you can collect it for yourself. Now, keep in mind that you are responsible for all of this equipment, you will sign for it and you will be receiving even more equipment such as a rucksack, Kevlar vest, compass, land navigation equipment and other things you will need during your ten weeks of training.

Around this time or maybe even before the inventory is done, you will be given a phone call. Don't get to excited yet, this phone call is mandatory and it is scripted. You will call someone you trust to answer the phone and will relay a message to him or her. You will say something along these lines: "Hi (person you are calling) I made it to basic training safely and am about to begin my training. Be expecting letters from me and phone calls in the future. Good bye." And then you will hang up the phone. You won't be allowed to say anything more than this for this phone call but don't lose heart, you will have opportunities for phone calls again in the future. Keep in mind that training is only 10 weeks, not that long when you think about it. Once you are finished with your phone call your cell phones will be collected and only handed out again when you have earned a phone call or after you have graduated.

Now you will have a chance to store your gear in your lockers. (You will have to organize it on your own free time and there will be a specific way you have to organize it.) You will put a lock on your locker that has multiple keys, one of these keys you will give to the drill sergeant. This is so that if you ever lock yourself out of your locker you can go to the drill sergeant and ask them to open your locker for you. (Beware though, if you do have to go to the drill sergeant for your key the drill sergeant won't make it easy on you.) You and a battle buddy will probably end up carrying it up to the porch, get it unlocked and then carry it back to its proper place and those things are not light. I recommend hiding a key somewhere like under the padding of one of your boots and/or even give a battle buddy you trust an extra key. This way you will always have one available to you and can avoid the headache of going up to a drill sergeant and asking him to unlock your locker. A drill sergeant also has a key to your locker so that he can open your locker and look for contraband or other things depending on the situation but they will always be accompanied by two of your fellow battle buddies. Most of the time they want to go through your locker everyone will be in the bay and they'll tell you to open your lockers for an inspection. There are exceptions of course such as if someone was reported hiding a phone in their locker or if someone is in the hospital and need their C.A.C. out of their locker, the drill sergeant will then open that locker in the presence of two of your battle buddies and retrieve the necessary items.

Things to Know

(Figure 1) The Bay

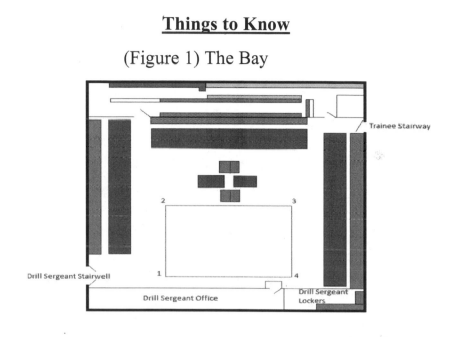

In figure 1 you will see a basic layout of what your bay may look like. Keep in mind that some drill sergeants like arrange things a little differently and the setup you go to could end up very different all together but the rules will remain the same. Everything I'm about to talk about will remain the same regardless of the setup.

Toeing the Line

The red box in the center is where you will be "toeing the line" You will line up in roster number order starting at the corner with the 1 in the diagram and going in a clockwise directing you will end at the 4 in the diagram. Never form up between the 4 and the 1. You will stand at the position of attention until someone calls "At ease" and then you will assume that position. This is where you will form up in the bay to receive instructions or lectures. My drill sergeants referred to this area as the "Kill Zone" because they said you were never allowed inside of it which is not entirely true. You are not allowed inside of it while you have been ordered to toe the line, and for the first few days to couple weeks you may not be allowed inside of the kill zone but eventually you will be seated in the kill zone for instructions, weapon maintenance, cleaning detail and numerous other activities. Eventually you will have a feel for when you're not allowed in the kill zone.

The Porch

There is a taped off area just outside the drill sergeant's office, this is known as the porch. As long as a cadre member remains in that box you don't need to say anything but whenever a cadre member having the rank of sergeant or higher (or higher rank than the cadre presently on the floor) steps out of the porch, the first one to notice it must call out in a loud voice "At ease" or in the case it's an officer you will call out: "Platoon. Attention!". At these commands everyone, no matter where they are or what they're doing must go to the position that was called out and face the direction the command came from. Also, at ease must be called whenever a sergeant enters the room from any door unless there is already a higher-ranking cadre member on the floor.

There will be times you need to speak with a drill sergeant and one is not present on the floor. In these cases, you must find a battle buddy, go up to the line of the porch (don't step over it) and knock on the door there will be instructions on what to do. Usually you will be told to knock two or three times loudly, and say "Drill Sergeant, (Your Rank, Your Last Name) requesting permission to speak with you Drill Sergeant." A cadre member will either open the door and you will be allowed to speak, or they will tell you to go away and come back later. If you don't have a battle buddy and a drill sergeant opens the door, be prepared to do pushups and then get a battle buddy.

Streamer Events

Every platoon will have their own phase banner with a guide arm bearer. The guide arm bearer is responsible for holding the banner whenever you leave your barracks. Your platoon can earn prestige by earning things called 'streamers'. Streamers are awards you receive for being the best in a specific event. The events that you can earn a streamer in varies for every company but I will list all the streamers that we were able to compete for in the two companies I was a part of. Remember prestige points are not only a form of friendly competition, but they also make you and your drill sergeants look good and when the drill sergeants look good they are more inclined to reward you. Sometimes the reward may come in the form of a 5-minute phone call or they may allow you to go to sleep 30 min earlier than normal. It's all up to the drill sergeant if they choose to give you a reward at all.

The streamers we were allowed to compete in were: Physical Fitness Test (P.T. Streamer), Obstacle course, Confidence course, Leadership course, Marksmanship, Grenades, Land Navigation, NIC at Night, Final Inspection and a final streamer given to the platoon with the most streamers to set them apart from everyone else. You may see all of these and more or you may only see a few of these.

Smoke Session/ Smoking/ Volunteer P.T.

There will be times when the drill sergeants will 'smoke' you and what this means is that you will be put through a rigorous exercise routine. Typically, these will consist of pushups, sit-ups and jumping, pushing you past the limits you thought you had. Smokings are used as both punishment and as way to get you into better shape. There are several terms that can be used interchangeably, 'smoking' is probably the most common however sometimes they may call it something else such as 'voluntary P.T.' no matter what they call it though you won't like it. I was surprised at how creative they could make a smoke session too! One drill sergeant smoked us until we were able to raise the temperature 3 degrees with the AC unit on. Another drill sergeant took a deck of cards and he would ask someone what the next card was. If we got it right, we were done, if we got it wrong, each card suit was assigned an exercise (e.g. diamonds were diamond pushups) and had a value assigned to it telling you how many you had to do. Other times they would smoke us while they lectured us about what we did wrong earning us that smoking. (Incidentally, the worse smoking I ever received was when someone from my platoon called our female drill sergeant 'mam' instead of 'drill sergeant'. She smoked us for a good long while and just as she was finishing, another drill sergeant came in and asked why we were getting smoked. After we told him the reason he decided to smoke us as again.)

Chow

For chow you will be marched over to a mess hall where a drill sergeant will issue commands to each platoon or to the entire company. There will be two lines inside the chow hall to get your food, the food is usually the same on both sides but sometimes one line will have something the other doesn't or in place of. While in line you will pick up a tray and silverware, do not forget either or you will be made an example of. Usually this will consist of standing between to the two lines and shouting loud and clear "Don't forget your silverware" over and over. Once you get to the counter where the food is you will place your tray on the sliding rail and sidestep the rest of the way through the line. If you are lucky and can choose your food, do it quickly and move on. Once you've received your hot food you will proceed to the salad bar, there will be salad, fruits, vegies, sunflower seeds, cottage cheese, salad dressing and sometimes peanut butter and jelly typically. There may even be cake but you do not want to touch that! You will then collect what you need and get into another line to collect your drinks. You will be given two glasses of a flavorless sports drink and you will be required to drink both glasses! Dehydration is dangerous and you will need those electrolytes.

You will then proceed to an empty spot at a table. (You cannot pick the table, you will go to a table that is filling up and if it's filled all the way then you go to the next empty table.) You may be required to stand holding your tray until your table is fill and then sit, or you may be allowed to just sit and start eating. Regardless of the procedure you're given, when you do sit down, eat fast! "Eat now, taste it later!" is what the drill sergeants would tell us, or "Food is fuel, fill up fast!" Also, when eating, do not look around and do not talk, if a drill sergeant sees you talking or looking around he will go to the table and tell everyone they're done eating. It won't matter if you sat down two minutes ago, you will be done. Assuming you don't have any idiots at your table, you will have about ten minutes to eat your food and drink your drinks. At the end of your meal you will stand up with your tray and take it to a person who will be collecting the trays or place your empty tray in a designated area and form up by platoon outside.

Lights Out

Lights out is exactly what is sounds like, bed time. This is when the drill sergeants will tell you to turn off the lights and get into bed. Most of the drill sergeants will go home at this time to catch a few hours of sleep themselves, except for the one pulling CQ and Staff duty. Once the lights go out everyone is expected to be in bed and sleeping in your P.T. uniform. Sometimes you will have people talking, horsing around, or even going into the latrine to read or write letters. Do not get caught doing these things because the CQ sergeant will be making the rounds and if he catches anyone out of bed without a legitimate excuse he can punish not only you but your entire platoon. Punishments are dependent on the drill sergeant, it can be something simple like just telling you to get back to bed, he could have you take the next CQ shift in place of someone else or he could wake the entire bay up to do a smoke session. It rarely goes to the extreme of waking the bay up, but I have had a drill sergeant threaten to do just that.

Fire Guard

Every bay I've been to has had the fire guard desk placed someplace different. Some will have it in the kill zone, some will have it near the drill sergeant stairwell and others will have it in some random out of the place area. It doesn't matter where the desk is because when you're on fireguard you will be either cleaning, making the rounds, writing reports or writing letters. Fireguard consists of two people per shift in one-hour shift increments. Your battle buddies will create a schedule (usually going in roster number order repeating itself). While on fireguard one of you will man the fireguard desk and keep a record of everything that goes on. If someone that doesn't belong to your bay or a cadre member comes through, you'll write down that event and the time that it happened. If one of your battle buddies needs to use the latrine they'll come up to you and leave you their dog tags, which you will write down in your report as well. You'll write down their roster number, put latrine and the time they went and the time they came back. You will also write down the count of everybody that is currently in their bunks and when you have weapons assigned to you, you write down the count of the weapons.

The other person pulling fireguard with you will be walking around and actually doing the counting of the weapons and reporting it to the one sitting at the desk. They will then walk around and take a head count to make sure nobody has tried to sneak in or out of the bay. They will also have a cleaning task that the platoon has assigned. (My platoon would assign little cleaning duties for each shift such as sweeping the bay for one shift, mopping the bay, sweeping the latrine, mopping the latrine, clean the sinks etc.)

The two battle buddies performing fireguard will swap positions about half way through, and then about 10 min prior to the next shift, they will wake up the next fireguard so they can get ready and relieve you on time. You will also have to wake C.Q. for their shift if your platoon has the C.Q. shift. If your platoon has staff duty you will want to wake them up at least twenty to thirty minutes early because they will need to get dressed in the proper uniform and they really don't want to be late.

Different drill sergeants have different requirements for the uniform you are required to wear, most allow you to wear your P.T. uniform along with your camelback and your flashlight with a red lens for fireguard and C.Q. If you're the last shift on fireguard duty, you will also be responsible for turning on the lights at the correct time in order to wake everyone up. The last shift will also be the ones taking out the bay's trash and running the mail over to the mailbox. (These end of shift duties will vary by what the drill sergeants allow.)

C.Q.

Charge of Quarters (C.Q.) duty is done at the same time as fireguard. Usually, which ever drill sergeant has C.Q. will have their platoon pull the shift. Again, the uniform will be decided by the drill sergeant on C.Q. and it will typically be announced at the meeting that takes place after dinner.

Sometimes you'll find hold overs (soldiers that were injured or are unable to continue training) manning this desk during the day. If you get an opportunity to speak with them, they will be more than happy to talk to you about what to expect and answer any other questions you may have. These trainees will also typically have the latest private news network (PNN) gossip if you're hungry for that kind of thing.

Staff Duty

Night:

Staff duty will be held at the same time as fireguard and is located in the battalion office. Here you will need to be dressed in your army uniform and you must arrive at least five minutes early to receive turnover and instructions. While on staff duty your duties will vary, you and your battle buddy may simply sit in a chair for the duration of your shift or you may be asked to sit behind the desk, answer the phone and take messages for a drill sergeant when necessary. You may also be asked to clean the latrine, sweep the hallways or even clean the classrooms.

It's very important to be alert in this area because this is the area is where a lot of officer's work, they may come in asking you questions or just pass by you on the way to their office. The important thing to remember is your military bearing and if someone does speak with you remember to be very respectful. If they're not in uniform it could still be someone important and even if they're just a civilian you are representing the US Army. Once your shift is over and you have been relieved you will return to the barracks, change back into your P.T. uniform and get what sleep you can. If you are the last shift, wait for a drill sergeant to release you before you return.

When I would prepare for staff duty I would go to bed in my Army Uniform so when I was woken up, all I had to do was grab my camelback and put on my boots. I also kept covered up with a blanket while I slept so that if a drill sergeant happened to walk by my bunk he/ she wouldn't see what I was wearing.

Day:

Day Staff Duty will usually be done by hold overs and consists of the same duties as the night shift however there will be a greater number of people working there and, several of them will even be civilians. You will be answering questions such as 'Where is the cornel's office?' or 'Where is S3?' and even 'Where is the on-duty drill sergeant?'. You will also receive phone calls asking you for information such as where a certain soldier is located, and if you should get a call like this you will take a message containing the soldiers information that they are looking for, who is looking for him, if they can tell you why they are looking for this soldier, you will take that down and you will ask for a call back number. After you have all of this information you will inform them that the information will be given to the drill sergeant in charge and that he or she will take care of it. You will then contact the drill sergeant in charge of the staff duty desk and inform him or her of the call. The staff duty sergeant will leave a way of contacting them or they will inform you where they will be in the event such a call does occur. There are no time limits as to how long you can remain on staff duty as a hold over, I myself once pulled a 16-hour shift, only breaking for meals. One advantage to being there though is you can get to know a lot of other people, including the battalion commander. While I was there I got to know the battalion commander much better than I would have otherwise and found him to be a great guy, he earned my respect in both rank and as a person. While performing staff duty you will encounter civilians, privates, NCO's and officers of all ranks, be respectful to all of them.

Ammo Guard

There may be times when your company will have ammunition that needs to be stored outside and when that happens it must be guarded. This is actually a pretty easy task as you will be sitting in a chair and making sure no one goes near the ammo. You'll be keeping your eyes open for an NCO and any officers still and an ammo guard will be posted all night just like C.Q. (Although sometimes C.Q. gets ammo guard as an additional duty.) If there are any injured soldiers or hold overs, they can be put on ammo guard during the training portion of the day. I remember spending quite a bit of time out on ammo guard as a hold over, especially on Sundays.

Bay Maintenance

You will be required to keep your bay clean and you will be expected to clean it daily. In the morning before you get ready for P.T. you will have to make your bed. Your boots, shoes and flip flops will be under your bed in a neat line arranged in the said order. If you're on the top bunk your shoes will go on the opposite side of the bed your bunk mate is on. Your locker will be closed and locked. There will be two metal hangers hanging from your locker, one will have a neatly folded towel and the other will have a clean P.T. uniform. Everything mentioned above must be uniform, meaning it must look identical to everyone else. You will also need to make sure you take out the trash in the morning and make sure the fireguard lights have been turned off.

In the evening after you've finished your last meal for the day you will be given a little free time before lights out. One of the first things your platoon should do is divide the bay into groups (easiest to go by roster numbers, maybe 10 – 15 per group. The first group or two will clean the latrine, the toilets need to be cleaned good, the showers scrubbed down (every three weeks maybe take the curtains outside and scrub them good.) The sinks have to be cleaned as well as the mirrors, the floor needs to be swept and mopped. If there are things in the latrine like forgotten towels or something, create a lost and found box (if you have access to one) and store it somewhere out of the way, maybe like the cleaning closet. Have another group sweeping the entire bay (excluding the latrine) this includes around the shoes, under the bunks, where ever they can get a broom. Another group will need to mop the floor. Have one group clean up other things such as wiping down the vents, the fire extinguisher, tops of doors, tops of lockers etc.

Remember, that one shoe out of place, or one person's towel folded wrong is more than enough of a reason to have the bay torn apart by a drill sergeant.

Bed Making

First, have your bed fully stripped. Start by placing your first sheet on your bed. Odds are your sheet won't cover your entire bed, so for the first sheet you'll pull it up to where your pillow is. Make sure it's even on both sides and pull it far enough toward the head of your bed to tuck that side under the mattress. You will then make the hospital corner nearest the pillow end of your bed. Do the same on the other side and tuck the rest of the sheets under the mattress.

Now for the second sheet, you'll do the exact same side but for the rear end of the bed. For the blanket you'll start by turning your pill so it's long ways on your bed. Place your blanket on your bed making sure the end goes only as far as your pillow, and tuck the sides under the bed, not forgetting the hospital corners at the one end. Make sure the blanket is as tight as you can get it.

TIP: If you're given a second blanket or are allowed to sleep in your sleeping bags I suggest you use them to sleep on top of your made bed. This way, in the morning all you have to do is put away the sleeping bag/ extra blanket and tighten your bed blankets down a along with your sheets and you've saved yourself a lot of time in the morning. (I suggest you look up how to make hospital corners before you go to basic but if you don't then ask someone once you arrive.)

Your platoon will have a linen day where you will strip your bed of all linin and will sort them into two different piles, sheets in one pile, pillow cases in another. Before P.T. that morning they will then be taken down to where you form up and you will have a designated area to place them. Later in the day you'll receive clean linin and will have to make your bed on your free time.

Laundry

Your platoon will be told when it can do laundry, it will probably have two or three days a week in which it has access to the laundry room. On these days you will wait until it's your 'free time' and take your laundry and soap down and wash / dry it. There are various ways your platoon may choose to do this:

1. Everyone is responsible for their own laundry and you get it done yourself.
2. Someone or a squad of people is responsible for doing everyone's laundry in the bay and getting it back to them.
3. Half the platoon (everyone on bottom bunks) goes down to do laundry and they do their battle buddies laundry as well, and then the next week it switches.

Mail Call

Getting letters from friends and loved ones can mean everything to you and each letter is worth its weight in gold. For us, mail would come in and be collected throughout the week and could be distributed to us on any day of the week, usually only once a week though. If you're getting a package, the drill sergeants will open the package in front of everyone with you and inspect it for contraband. If your letters feel like they may have something inside of them like pictures, they will have you open the letter in front of them to make sure there are no 'inappropriate pictures' and if there are, they will escort you to a shredder where you will destroy them.

Postal Exchange

From time to time your company will march down to the P.X. to stalk up on hygiene supplies and other necessary items you may need. If you have the opportunity and if its allowed I recommend buying a bore snake for cleaning your rifle, Fox river socks because they're thicker and are much better than the socks you're issued. On these trips to the P.X. you'll also be getting a haircut. Drill sergeants will inform you of what you are and are not allowed to buy. If you feel like splurging a little you can purchase water proof notepads, better pens and other fancy things for basic training. This is also the time you should stock up on envelopes and stamps if you don't have enough.

Red Phase

Rifle

In your first week of training you'll receive your rifle. (M-16 or M-4) You will line up in roster number order and be called one at a time to come and pick up your rifle. When you pick it up you will ensure that the safety selector is on safe and then you will verify the serial number is the same as on the paper. Once this is done you will sign your name and move on. When you return to your bay you will be attaching the blank firing adapter (BFA) at the end of the barrel. The most important thing to remember is to always maintain control over your rifle and don't let it point at anyone! When your rifle's barrel is pointed at someone it's called "Flagging" and if a drill sergeant catches you flagging someone, expect to get yelled at and to do pushups. If you flag a drill sergeant you can expect a much harsher punishment. If you drop your rifle you can also expect to do pushups with the rifle laying across your hands.

You will be instructed on how to hold your weapon, how to check it, how to fire it, and how to maneuver it in drill and ceremony. You will use these skills throughout basic training and you will be tested on them over and over.

On the side of your weapon you will have a serial number, memorize it if you can, at the very least write it down in your notebook so you can always identify your weapon. You will probably be instructed to place a piece of colored tape on the buttstock of your rifle and write your roster number on it. (Some of my battle buddies would also stick a piece of tape on the other side of their buttstock and name their weapon. If you do this be prepared to take it off if the drill sergeants don't like it. They want everyone to be uniform and customizing your weapon is not being uniform with everyone else.)

Always make sure your weapon is clean. A dirty weapon can jam up easily and fail to fire and you always want your weapon to fire perfectly. Also, be very careful with your weapons parts making sure not to lose them or get them mixed up with anyone else's. Despite all of rifles looking alike, all of the parts are specifically made for your weapon. Your firing pin for example, is filed down to a specific point to work in your rifle and will not work in anyone else's rifle.

4 Tennent's:

- Always treat every weapon as if it was loaded
- Never point your weapon at anything you don't intend to shoot
- Always keep your weapon on safe unless you are going to squeeze the trigger
- Always keep your finger outside the trigger well unless you are going to shoot

Clearing procedure:
- Attempt to put your weapon on safe
- Remove the magazine
- Pull the Charging handle to the rear and lock the bolt to the rear
- Check for ammo
- Release bolt

Fundamentals of Marksmanship:
- Steady Position
- Breathing

- Relax
- Aiming
- Trigger squeeze

8 Cycles of Function

- Feeding
- Chambering
- Locking
- Firing
- Unlocking
- Extracting
- Ejecting
- Cocking

__M-16 / M-4__

The M-16 / M-4 rifle is:

- Magazine fed
- Gas operated
- Air cooled
- Shoulder fired
- 5.56 mm
- Can be fired in semi or 3 round burst

In the event of a jam you will perform S.P.O.R.T.S:

- Slap   (Slap the magazine up)
- Pull   (Pull back the charging handle all the way back)
- Observe   (Look down the ejection port and look into the area for any ammo or obstructions in the chamber)
- Release   (Release the charging handle)
- Tap   (Tap the forward assist button)
- Squeeze   (Squeeze the trigger)

Land Navigation

In land navigation you are going to learn how to navigate from one point to another point using a map, a compass, a protractor, a pencil and your wits. You will be shown how to read a map properly, what the different colored lines on a map stand for and how to read the edges of a map. You will also learn how to read grid coordinates and draw a line on map and calculate the distance. You will sit through several long classes and even longer power point presentations. Once the presentations are over though, the drill sergeants will want to make sure that you know what you're doing and they will give you points to plot on your map and put you though several in class exercises. If you are having any trouble understanding anything let the drill sergeants know and they will help you. This is one of those rare times where they will actually act friendly, they don't want to scare you right now because they know how important this section is. I spoke with several drill sergeants on different points of land navigation and they were happy to explain things to me.

Once you have the basics down you will need to do a pace count, this consist of you walking a certain distance (usually 100 meters) and you will count how many steps it took you. You will then do this again at a jogging pace. When doing these pace counts, make sure they're natural steps or a steady jogging pace you could keep up for long distances if needed. You will be using your pace count when you are asked to find different locations during the land navigation course so write them down somewhere. I wrote mine down on the inside of my patrol cap.

You will be bussed out to a location where you will be teamed up with another member of your platoon. You will then be given a pencil, a map, a protractor and a compass. Each group will be given a piece of paper with around 5 coordinates on it which you will need to plot on your map. (Each piece of paper will have different coordinates on it.) It's not necessary to follow the order of the coordinates when plot them and the points are usually random so it would be best for you to take the most efficient route to hit all of the points. You will be given a time limit for how long you can search for these points and you must be back before the allotted time comes to an end. Each coordinate will have a marker and the markers will have something that you need to write down in order to get credit for finding that coordinate. There could be up 4 or more things written on each marker, you won't write everything down, only the side of the marker indicated by your paper. (e.g. each side of the marker is labeled A, R, M, Y, and under A will be LDR, and under R will be SGT and so forth. If your paper asks you for what's under R, you will write SGT.)

The object is to obtain as many of these coordinates as possible and return to your starting location with the fastest time. Land navigation can also be a streamer event for which you will be competing. The drill sergeants have several criteria for judging this, they may choose to go by who found the most points in the allotted time, they may judge by points and time, they may judge by people who failed to return in the given time. Just do your best and try to have fun while you're out there.

The Land navigation course will be done twice, once during the day and then again at night. The day course is pretty easy and if you have any trouble on the course you can generally look around and see where other people are gathering, it's usually at a marker. Finding a coordinate marker is always good even if it isn't one of yours because if it's yours then you can mark it off and if it's not yours you can use it to find out where you are and get a new baring on where your marker is. You can also listen for where other groups of people and follow those sounds or look for worn trails from all the foot traffic to the markers. During the day time it's easy to find your coordinates, but during the night it's going to be a little harder.

For the night land navigation course, you will first be told to put your red lenses on your flashlight. Like before you will be given several coordinates and you will go find them in a given time limit. You will be told to use the flashlights as little as possible because light can easily be seen by anyone and you are trying to avoid detection.

There's a decent chance you will be staying the night out here unless the weather prohibits an overnight stay. This will be considered one of your field training exercises (FTX) and sleeping out in the field is not always fun. When you go to bed down for the night you will form a perimeter (your platoon or squad leaders will instruct you on where to go) and you will have to pull guard duty during the night. The drill sergeants will tell you what kind of security you're going to pull, you could be pulling 100% security where everyone stays up, you could be told you're pulling 50% security where your battle buddy will sleep for one hour, then wake you up and you guard for one hour and keep repeating this cycle. Or it could be something like every other position will guard for an hour or 2 and then wake the next group. All of this will be explained in detail before you go to bed. When you're pulling guard though, you will in the long halt position watching for signs of the enemy and there could be enemies! Drill sergeants will patrol looking for gaps in the defense or people sleeping on the job and they will… make life a lot less pleasant for you.

Remember, always mind your surroundings, watch for spider webs, snakes, wild animals, obstructions such as barbed wire, old knives, empty cans left over from MRE's and other such things that could injure you. The drill sergeants will give you more details about any dangers in the area to be aware of.

Medical Training

At some point, usually in red phase but can anywhere in your training, you will have some medics come into your bay or a classroom and teach you how to perform basic first aid. You should have an improved first aid kit (IFAK) with you, and inside it will be some general first aid equipment such as a tourniquet, some gauss and a few other things that you will get instructed on how to use. You will be shown how to stop a major wound from bleeding out and how to mark them so a medic knows the situation. You will also be shown the proper ways to carry an injured soldier off the battlefield using several different methods. Some of the different types of carries may be asked on your red phase testing, but most of the testing will be done outside where you do P.T. in the mornings. The testing will consist of you demonstrating several or all of the carries. For some of them you will be using a sled to pull someone or using a stretcher to carry someone else. You will be instructed on who is in charge when giving commands and what commands to give are.

(We were instructed to attach our IFAK to our camelback and since we had it with us all of the time we would stick a little extra paper inside and a couple of pens and if we had room we could store profiles and a few other things inside of them as well.)

Radio Training

In red phase you will receive some radio training. You will learn how to assemble a radio, how to program it and how to talk on it. The radio you will most likely be learning on will be an Advance System Improvement Program (ASIP) Receiver / Transmitter. At this time, you'll also learn how to do a 9-line medevac request.

9 Line Medevac

1. Location of the pick-up site
2. Radio frequency, call sign, and suffix
3. Number of patients by precedence:
   A – Urgent
   B – Urgent Surgical
   C – Priority
   D – Routine
   E – Convenience
4. Special equipment required:
   A – None
   B – Hoist
   C – Extraction equipment
   D – Ventilator
5. Number of patients:
   A – Litter
   B – Ambulatory
6. Security at pick-up site:
   N – No enemy troops in area
   P – Possible enemy troops in area

E – Enemy troops in area
X – Enemy troops in area

7. Method of marking pick-up site:
   A – Panels
   B – Pyrotechnic signal
   C – Smoke signal
   D – None
   E – Other

8. Patient nationality and status:
   A – US Military
   B – US Civilian
   C – Non-US Military
   D – Non-US Civilian
   E – EPW

9. NBC Contamination:
   N – Nuclear
   B – Biological
   C – Chemical

The radio training and 9-line medevac could be on your red phase test. You may also find yourself using an ASIP on fireguard to make your reports to the CQ desk.

Rappelling

If you have a fear of heights you have my sympathies because you will be facing those fears on a 40 ft. rappelling wall. This training could take up to the whole day, going right after breakfast and staying there until dinner. You will begin with a safety brief followed by getting broken down into groups. When it's your groups turn you will be taken to a station where you will learn how to put on your safety harness. When putting on the safety harness it should be tight and a little uncomfortable. You will then be sent to a miniature tower where you will be about five feet off the ground, several drill sergeants will be instructing you on how far to lean back and how to rappel.

Once you're done with this you will climb up a ladder to the top of the rappelling tower and crawl to a set point and wait until a drill sergeant calls you over. There will be several drill sergeants on the wall waiting for you, and when you go over to them they will ensure you are properly connected and will issue you instructions. They will tell you to stand on the ledge first and then have you lean back. Next, they will have you do a few small jumps where you stay in place and when they're satisfied with your jumps they will tell you to rappel down. You can easily rappel down the 40 ft. wall in three good bounds, and once you're done you'll realize that it was fun and find yourself wishing you could do it again. When you reach the bottom you will remove the ropes from your harness and take the ropes away from your spotter, pull them all way out and untangle them. You will be the spotter for the next person and that person will take your spot as a spotter. When your turn as a spotter is over you will then remove your harness and return it to where you got it.

You're not quite done here yet, there may be a few other obstacles you will be doing as well like climbing up a wall at a slight angle using just your feet and a rope to help pull yourself up, climb a few other minor obstacles and climb down a cargo net.

Obstacle / Confidence / Leadership Courses

Leadership Reaction Course (LRC)

The leadership course is perhaps the most fun out of all the courses you will do. Here you will work in groups of 4 – 7 people to complete obstacles. These obstacles are essentially puzzles that will require teamwork, cunning and someone leading the team on what to do. While many of the puzzles are similar to each other they will each have one annoying obstacle you will have to think outside the box to overcome. Most of them will involve making bridges or getting across a body of water without getting wet. (This is a really good time to make use of those zip lock bags I was telling you to bring in case you should fall into the water.) There is a way to complete every obstacle and sometimes there are several ways to complete them. I will admit that we failed several of the courses but everyone had something to contribute. If you have an idea on how to complete a puzzle, then voice it. If there are several ideas, vote on them and try the one that wins, if it doesn't work out, try the next idea. You may be a leader in one, several or even all of them, but listen to everyone's ideas.

Obstacle Course

The obstacle course is designed to physically test you individually. A drill sergeant will take you through each obstacle and demonstrate the right and a comical wrong way of doing each obstacle. You will be competing on the obstacle course by platoon. Your obstacle course may consist of a ditch you will crawl through, a rope you will climb, monkey bars, a rope you will jump up and grab and placing your legs over the rope and pulling yourself to the other end, jumping over a wall, crawling over a wall keeping a low profile, crawling under a wall or through a fence, running over a wooden beam, dropping into a ditch into water and getting out of the ditch, crawling under barbed wire and finally crawling through a concrete tube. (This was my obstacle course, yours may have different obstacles in store for you.) Your platoon will be timed to see how fast they can complete the entire obstacle course, taking into account penalties for those that can't do a specific obstacle. Once the times are all accounted for the platoon with the fastest time will receive a streamer.

(If one of your battle buddies is struggling, don't be afraid to give moral support!)

Confidence Course

The confidence course is not the same as the obstacle course but there are similarities. The confidence course is a series of obstacles but unlike the obstacle course, some of them will require teamwork to complete.

The most memorable obstacle for me was a four-leveled tower where four of you will climb the tower helping each other to each reach the next level of the tower. Each level increases in height, for example, the distance between the 1st level and the 2nd may be 5'6", and between 2nd and 3rd may be 6', and 6;6" for the last.

Another team work obstacle are the walls. I don't know if they had an official name, but they are a series of walls, each one increasing in height. What happens here is you will have a team of 3 -5 people and you will have to get over each wall. One person will boost the others up onto the wall while two would remain on the top of the wall to help pull the person still on the ground up. One of my companies actually had us timed and the platoon with the best time was awarded a streamer for this.

Another obstacle I remember is a series of obstacles rolled into one. First, you'll climb a rope about 15 -20 feet off the ground, you will then walk across a beam about 4 inches wide and distance of about 10 feet. (There are safety nets if you should fall) You will then climb a ladder about 10 feet up and you will crawl over the edge where there is a rope cargo net going all the way down. Maintaining three points of contact you will climb all the way down until you're about three feet from the bottom, at this point you will cross your arms over your chest and allow yourself to fall onto the mat below.

The next obstacle of note is Jacobs Ladder, here you will climb a ladder like structure (Always maintaining 3 points of contact while climbing) until you get to a point where a drill sergeant is waiting (or a point instructed by a drill sergeant) crawl over and climb back down.

The next obstacle is the weaver. The weaver looks like monkey bars that go up and then come back down like a triangle that's about 7 feet wide by twenty feet long. Here you will sit on the first bar, go under the second bar and pull yourself up onto the second bar so that you are sitting on it. You will then repeat this for every bar all the way up and all the way down. You can grab other bars to help you get back up, you can use your legs and toss them on the third bar to help you up even. Anything goes as long as you're not receiving any help from anyone and you're not touching the ground.

The next obstacle is come to is a log that is about five feet off the ground in a vertical state. While running at the log you will place both hands on the log and jump over it by swinging both your legs over one side of the log. Remember to jump over the log, I only say this because one of my battle buddies ran straight into the log cracking one of his ribs. It took the rest of the cycle for him to heal and when he finally did heal up, he had to restart the next cycle from day zero.

The next obstacle are the balancing logs where you will simply balance on a log as you walk across them. The balancing log is implemented into several obstacles that you may or may not get the chance to do.

You will find another dozen or so smaller obstacles that require no supervision unlike the first 6 that I mentioned. You may not have time to do all of these because of the time frame you're scheduled to be on the course. The first time I did this course, I ran the whole course about 3 times before we were done, whereas when I was with my second company, we barely had time to get the first six done before we had to pack up and leave.

Gas Chamber

The gas chamber is an experience that just can't be put into words, you have to experience it. I was looking forward to trying the gas chamber since the day I signed my contract and now that I've done it, I have no desire to go through it again. It's actually not that bad, but once is enough of an experience for anyone. Going through the gas chamber serves two purposes, the first and most obvious to most people is to get exposed to gas and see how it can affect you. If you are ever exposed to a situation with gas you will know what to expect and so you will be better able to control your fear and react properly. The second purpose of the gas chamber and equally important, is feeling comfortable with and trusting your equipment to keep you safe.

Before going to the gas chamber though, you will be issued a gas mask with filters. You will be shown the proper way to put your mask on and how to make sure you have a solid seal. You will be timed on how fast you can put your mask on and get a proper seal, even though you are not tested on it the drill sergeants want you to be able to put the mask on in a given amount of time. You will also learn the different signals warning you that you need to put your mask on.

The day you go to the gas chamber you will be dropped off at a site and given a safety brief. Following the briefing you will undergo a thorough inspection of your equipment. You will put on your gas mask and someone will be going around making sure that you have a solid seal on your mask before you can get in line to go into the gas chamber. When your group is ready to go up to the gas chamber the drill sergeants will have you do some exercises, maybe jogging in place or running around the building a few times. What they want is for you to be sweating and winded for when you go inside. Once you are deemed ready, you'll be told to put your masks on and you will enter the gas chamber.

Inside the gas chamber you will stand where they tell you and they will set off a controlled amount of chlorobenzylidene-malononitrile (CS) gas, you have probably heard of it by its more common name, tear gas. The drill sergeants will ensure that your mask is working properly once the gas gets going. When everybody's mask has been verified to have a working seal you will be instructed to pull the mask away from you face, open your eyes and take a couple of breaths in, inhaling the gas. You will then return the mask to your face, create a proper seal and you will blow out as much you as can, pushing the CS gas out and breathing filtered air in. You may or may not start to feel a burning, different people have different tolerances for the gas. In my group, one person's mask didn't work and was told he could leave and do this again with a proper gas mask or he could stay and just bear with it. He stayed and the gas never affected him, while others were having trouble just taking in a couple of breaths. You will be told to take your mask off several times during your stay and you may be required to say the soldier's creed or give your full name, rank and platoon name before being allowed to put it back on. Eventually everyone will remove their mask entirely for a timed duration of one or two minutes before being allowed to exit the building.

Do not run out of the building! There are several reasons for this, first being safety. When you come out of the building you will be crying from the gas in your eyes and you don't want to be running over battle buddies or tripping over someone. Second, I've heard stories from older soldiers that went through basic training and at their gas chamber there was a three about three feet away from the exit door. When soldiers would rush out they would hit the tree, sometimes knocking them out. I was also told that, the tree just mentioned was bare of bark on the one side. (The story about that tree comes from a training facility in CA and is no longer used for basic training.)

Once you're out of the building you will need to start flapping your arms up and down at a steady pace while walking. If you need to throw up, you can do that (it makes for a great photo op for the photographers that will be there) but try to keep moving. By flapping your arms and moving you are getting fresh airing out your uniform thus removing any residual CS gas. Do not rub your eyes! You will have CS gas all over your body and rubbing your eyes will just make them hurt more.

I.E.D. Course

For the Improvised Explosive Device (IED) course you will be taken out to a field where a drill sergeant will explain to you what IED's are, how easily they can be constructed and how to spot a possible IED. After you've been briefed you will be allowed to go around to the different stations and learn about different types of IED's. There may be some stories told about I.E.D. from some of the drill sergeants. I was not tested over any of this but they wanted to make sure we were aware of what to look for.

Ruck March

Ruck marching isn't really all that hard once you've done the short one and figure out the pacing and a good breathing technique. There should be 2 -3 ruck marches per phase.

For the first one you'll be told to fill your Assault pack or your Ruck sack with certain gear. I can't say which gear because it didn't seem to really matter so much for the first few rucks, the drill sergeants just wanted your packs to be a little heavy to get you ready for the harder stuff later. Don't let what I just said make you think you can just pack a sleeping bag to make it look heavy, a drill sergeant may ask you to pack something specific like your canteen filled with water and have you pull it out as proof that you did in fact pack it. Aside from integrity, you'll also want to pack everything because you could end up staying the night somewhere if they decide to have you do a FTX. Some additional things you'll want to bring, ordered or not, is your wet weather bag and inside of that you'll want an extra pair of socks and an extra shirt. In one of your pockets that you can reach quick and easy, I would recommend stuffing a washcloth in there so that when you're marching you will have something to wipe the sweat off your face.

You'll be ordered to wear your flick, a flashlight using the red lens, your most comfortable pair of boots, your camelback (which can typically be attached to the back of or near the top of your assault / ruck sack. Make sure your camelback is filled with water because you will sweat a lot on these ruck marches.

There's a chance the regular morning PT will be cancelled on days you have a ruck march, this is because you will have a long day ahead of you and they don't want you tired out during the ruck, you will still do a series of stretching exercises right before the ruck begins though.

Just before the actual ruck march begins, you will form up and you'll be divided into two lines, each line will march on a different side of the road. You will have the job of scanning your side of the road for hazards, enemy combatants, IED's etc. (You'll most likely not see anything on any ruck march however, a drill sergeant may set things up for you to notice and if it's not reported in a timely manner... well then you can expect a rough time in the bay when you return.)

While your marching you will also be watching for hand signals from the drill sergeants or from your fellow trainees. Once you see the hand signal you will pass the signal along to the person behind you and take the required action. (The drill sergeants will brief you and teach you what all of these signals are.) Periodically you will be stopping and taking a knee, aiming your weapon in front of you scanning the area directly in front of you for hostiles, this position can be held for around five minutes and is called a short halt. If it lasts longer, a long halt will be called and every other person will lower their weapon, remove their pack and place it on the ground in front of them. They will then reclaim their weapon taking a prone position with their weapon resting on the top of their pack and scanning the area for enemy hostiles. The person that was guarding you while you repositioned yourself is now going to go down in the same position you're in. Once down every two people will cross ankles with each other, by doing this you can send messages back and forth to each other via pressure on the ankles. Usually the only message you'll be sending in training is, 'are you still awake?' For us, this signal was sent yy giving a quick amount of pressure on heel of the other person and they in turn responded the same way. It is very important that you make sure your battle buddies are awake though because after a long march it's easy to fall asleep in the prone position. If a drill sergeant catches you asleep you may find yourself doing some 'voluntary P.T.' later or even on the spot.

During a long halt, your squad leaders will come up to you and see if you have plenty of ammo and water. You will never have live ammo on a ruck march in basic training so you will always have the right amount of ammo when they ask. If you're running low on water though, let your squad leader know and he or she will refill your water source for you. On the note of ammo, some drill sergeants may have you chamber a blank round in your weapon and if they do, you need to be doubly cautious because if your weapon should fire for any reason while on a ruck march you can and most likely will be charged with negligent discharge of a weapon which can result in an Article 15. The purpose of the blank round is to make you more conscious about the weapon and to ensure you are using proper safety techniques.

Red Phase Test

Now it's time to be tested on the knowledge of everything you've been taught so far. In my first company, they made it an all-day event setting up tents the night before and dividing up the company into small manageable groups. Each group was sent to a specific station (or tent) where they would undergo testing of a specific area of knowledge. I remember one tent was a land navigation tent where you would plot points assigned to you specifically and you were asked several questions about land nav. Another tent was set up where one person would enter at a time and would be asked the chain of command and you were to tell them who each person was in the chain of command by looking at just a picture of that person. We were also told to recite the soldier's creed flawlessly. Another station had us perform morning P.T. exercises, you would be told which one to do and you had to perform it. Another was drill and ceremony with your rifle and I remember one being one being weapon knowledge where you they would give you a scenario and you would demonstrate how you would react in such an event explaining every step. We were given a paper and the drill sergeants would mark on them go or no-go and initial it. We were allowed one no-go, anything more and we would have to redo the stations we got no-go's on, or risk being recycled. This test was started right after breakfast and lasted until lunch.

On the other hand, the second company I was in the testing was a lot easier. Here we all toed the line in our bay and our drill sergeant asked random people random questions about what we had learned. If we got one wrong, we would start doing pushups until he/she was ready to ask the next question. That was really a stress-free test compared to the first one I had taken.

Your company will decide on how to test your knowledge, and they can quiz you on all of this at any time in the other phases. They seem to enjoy these pop quizes around meal time, while waiting to go into the mess hall. If you don't know your stuff, you may end up working up an even bigger appetite than when you got there.

White Phase

Congratulations on making it to white phase. White phase is mostly comprised of weapons training. You had an introduction to your weapon already at the start of red phase where I spoke about the fundamentals and by this time you will also have learned how to take it apart and clean it. Now you will put everything you've learned so far and everything you're about to learn into practice.

You or your drill sergeant will assign a platoon guide (PG) in this phase and in turn, he will assign squad leaders. This is now important because you have a new platoon chain of command. From now on if you have any questions or problems you will first speak to the squad leader you are assigned to. If they don't have the answers, they well go to the PG, and if the PG doesn't know he will go to the drill sergeants and ask. The PG is responsible for the platoon and if the platoon messes up, it's on him. The PG that is assigned can be there for the entire cycle if he's good but the PG isn't always a permanent position. A drill sergeant can fire a PG at any time for any reason. My first cycle my PG lasted the entire cycle while another platoons PG was fired and replaced every couple of days and in some cases, hours. In my second cycle we changed PG every two weeks to give others a chance at it. The PG will also be leading the platoon on marches to the mess hall when a drill sergeant isn't present and they will lead the platoon in cadences.

Your platoon may not get to go to the range every day because the drill sergeants may try to concentrate on half the company at a time out at the range. This allows them to give more one-on-one time with the soldiers and if there's a group that's having trouble, they can arrange the time to take this group to the range for extra training. The group that stays behind will probably be instructed in close combat training, do S.H.A.R.P. training, work on map reading or start discussing advanced tactics. Every day the groups will switch who goes and who stays. This isn't always the case though, the entire company may end up going to the range and in that case, you will be sitting on the bleachers most of the day waiting for your chance to shoot.

There are three positions you'll be required to fire from during your training. The first position is the prone supported, where you will rest the rifle on something like sandbags to help stabilize the weapon. The next position is the prone unsupported, where you will hold the rifle yourself while in the prone position. The third position is the kneeling position, where you will have one knee on the ground with that knee's foot behind you or under you, one knee in front of you with that foot planted firmly on the ground. You will use this knee to rest your elbow on for stability when aiming and firing your weapon.

You will train for 2 – 3 weeks on shooting your weapon, at first you will be zeroing your weapon. More often than not, this means you will work on your technique for shooting, your breathing, body position, trigger squeeze as well as setting up the rifle's sights to your specifications. A word of advice, find a position where your face is comfortable against the rifle when firing, take a good measurement of where your face is so that you can move it back there every time. This is known as getting your sight picture, if you should move where your head is when you fire, your sight picture will change and this will throw off your aim. I remember practicing and then marking where my nose would could touch the buttstock and taping a piece of a pipe cleaner there so that everything I went to take aim, I would have my nose touch the pipe cleaner and I knew I was in my sight picture.

Breathing is very important when firing your weapon, especially when in the prone position because a full breath of air will cause your rifle to aim down a little and exhaling all your air moves the rifle up a little. Find a time in your breathing to hold your breath, aim and fire. For me, I would aim my weapon at my target and let all of the air out of my lungs and then hold my breath for a few moments to fine adjust my aim and then squeeze the trigger. If I wasn't happy with something or I was running out of air I would relax, take a breath and exhale again and hold my breath. When I would exhale I would be in a pretty close position as when I last exhaled and it only took me about one or two seconds to line up a perfect shot. I felt exhaling all the air was best because your stomach was as flat as it was going to get and seemed to be a little more stable, but some people would fill their lungs all the way up and some would take a full breath in and the let half of it out before firing. All of these methods are correct and it's up to you to find which one works best for you.

Body position will vary depending on which position you're in, for the prone and prone supported, you will lay flat on your stomach, your legs spread about 45 degrees apart, your heel and your big toe should both be touching the ground, do not let your ankle be up in the air as this makes you less stable and when you're in the field, you don't want your ankle to get shot off. Better to learn good habits and kick bad ones from the start. While in the prone position you will be resting on your elbows, (when practicing in the bay I recommend getting out your elbow pads) You may or may not be allowed elbow pads out on the range, my first cycle it was required and my second cycle it was not allowed. In either case, when you can practice in the bay, use elbow pads and make it a little easier on yourself.

Trigger squeeze can be a little tricky and is equally important as breathing and body position. I know at first it may be hard to understand but you never pull the trigger on your weapon, you squeeze it. The best way I can put it is, imagine getting angry and you start tightening your hand into a fist, that is exactly what you should do. When you're thinking of it like that, you're not actually pulling the trigger, the trigger is being squeezed back as you tighten your fist. Finger placement on the trigger is also important and this is even harder to explain. I've heard people tell me to use the end of my finger to squeeze the trigger, others tell me the crease between the 'padding' on your fingers and others have told me to use the middle 'padding' of the second padded section of my finger. I myself, use the second padded section of my index finger. You will be told by your drill sergeant a finger placement but the finger placement for one person won't always work for another, so if you're struggling with your groupings, you could try changing your trigger finger placement to see if that helps.

Relax. Don't stress out about firing your weapon, it's only a tool and you are the one controlling it. Try to relax as much as you can when firing, your shots will be more accurate that way and you'll be able to enjoy firing your weapon at the same time. This is also why practicing is so important, the more comfortable you are with firing your weapon the more you'll be able to relax when you're firing live rounds.

Remember BRAS: Breath, Relax, Aim, Squeeze.

Here's an exercise if you're having doubts or trouble with your grouping. When you're practicing doing a dry fire (A dry fire is you'll aim and fire the weapon without the weapon being loaded.) take aim and have someone place a penny or some type of coin on the end of the barrel so that it's balancing, when you pull the trigger it should remain on the barrel, if it falls off you're moving to much when you pull the trigger (which will throw off your aim) and you will need to practice until you can fire without the coin falling off.

Some people have trouble because they anticipate the noise of the weapon they're about to fire and they'll jerk out because of it. If this happens to be you I have only one piece of advice. When you're going to fire your weapon let yourself be startled by the noise rather than trying to anticipate it. I don't know if this will help but when I aim and fire, I concentrate on just the target and don't let anything else bother me. Just you, the target and concentrating on the fundamentals, body position, breathing, relaxing, aiming and squeezing. If you're concentrating on all of that, you shouldn't have the time to worry about a little noise.

The Range

When you go to the range you'll want to remember your weapon, your helmet, your ear protection, eye protection, three magazines and elbow pads if you're allowed to use them. You will be shuttled out to a range where you will form up by platoon. You will be instructed to leave your assault bag behind and shotgun your weapon. (place the things you will not need in your assault bag including your blank firing adapter.) Shot gunning your weapon means you'll take the weapon partially apart, removing the bolt assembly and holding it over your shoulder so it should make an 'L' shape. You will then line up, with your bolt assembly in one hand while a drill sergeant inspects your barrel to ensure that it's clear. You will be given the go ahead and you will 'move with a purpose' to the bleachers. You will reassemble your weapon and sit on the bleachers; your weapons buttstock may rest on the floor in front of you but you may not rest your hand or anything on top of the weapons barrel. You will be given a safety brief every time you go to the range and you will be told how to enter and leave the firing range. (NOTE: When you are leaving the range, you must have your weapon checked at the clearing barrel by a drill sergeant or someone the drill sergeant has instructed to check for them. If there is no drill sergeant present at the clearing barrel, do not check your weapon yourself or have a battle buddy do it, simply wait for a drill sergeant, or hand your weapon to a battle buddy who will wait while you retrieve a drill sergeant. If you attempt to leave the area without it being checked you're in for a rough day.)

After the briefing is over you will be instructed on how to retrieve ammo and how many of you may go at a time. You will receive your ammo and proceed to a designated lane where you will lay your weapon on the ground in a designated area and load your ammo into your magazines. Once loaded you may place your magazines next to your weapon or you may hold them. You will be given around 15 - rounds, 3 - 5 rounds per magazine when grouping, depending on how many they want you to group and how many they want you to fire at a time. 20 rounds of ammo will go into one magazine and 10 in each of the remaining two magazines for qualifications.

When it's your turn to shoot, you will pick your weapon and magazines up, go over to the firing platform and lay your weapon and magazines down. (This is a good time to put your ear plugs in.) You will be instructed to get into a good firing position, this is when you will get into the prone supported firing position. You will then be told to load your weapon. You will then be told to move your firing switch from safe to Simi and fire when ready. (commands may vary.)

The first time you fire live round you will be shooting at a paper about 25 yards away with the goal of grouping your shots as closely together as possible and hitting center mass of the paper target. Once you've managed a good grouping and your sights have been adjusted to your sight picture, you will be given a go ahead and you will leave the firing area by way of the clearing barrel. You will then turn your paper target in and you will sit on the bleachers until you're told differently. (keep your voice down while on the bleachers, drill sergeants hate the additional noise and may decide that everyone on the bleachers could use additional P.T.) If you failed to get a good grouping you may receive some additional training and will have to try again.

For qualifications you will be firing at pop up targets that are at 50 yards all the way out to 300 yards in 50-yard increments and they will pop up at random for a given amount of time before going down. Sometimes two targets will pop up and you will have to hit them both in the given amount of time. Remember, you have only 40 rounds and 40 targets, so if you're having trouble with the 250 or 300-yard targets, don't waste additional shots trying to get them. Try and use one shot for every target. However, if you miss a 100-yard shot, it may be worth shooting at again and sacrificing a 300-yard shot that you may or may not get. Don't worry about keeping track of how many you knock down; the computers will keep count and you'll be told your score once you're off the range.

Once you're done firing for the day you will be told to go and collect all of the shell casings and pick up any trash. You'll then get into a formation (Not by your assault bags yet) and open ranks. You will empty everything out of your pockets and place them into your PC laying on the ground in front of you with your helmet and your weapon, including your dog tags. You will pull your firing handle back and lock it into place and hold your weapon above your head. A drill sergeant will then come up to you and you will say "No brass, no ammo!" and then turn your head to the side. A drill sergeant will pat you down (Usually they're not very gentle with it and they can knock you back if you're not prepared.) They will then check your weapon as well as go through your things looking for any ordinance (ammo) that you may have. Once they give you the go ahead you will put everything back on and you will be allowed to return to your assault bag. This will be done every time you handle ammo.

Close in Combat

At some point in white phase, usually when half the platoon is at the range, or if everyone goes, a set amount of time will be used to learn close combat. We were taught how to put people into submissive holds and how to escape holds, all of them being from a downed position. You may only have a few days of training in this and the training is meant for you to get up and out of a hold, retrieve your weapon and continue your mission.

White Phase Test

Your white phase test consists of your ability to qualify with your weapon and is conducted at weapons qualifications. For your weapons qualification you will be given 40 rounds of live ammunition which you will load into your 3 magazines. You will load 20 rounds into your first magazine and 10 rounds in the other two magazines. You will have to hit a minimum of 23 of the 40 targets that will pop up to achieve the lowest qualifying score. In addition to being your white phase test, this is also where you will earn a badge for your dress blues showing everyone what kind of a shot you are. 23 – 29 targets hit will earn you an Army marksmanship badge, 30 – 35 targets hit will earn you an Army sharpshooter badge and 36 – 40 targets hit will earn you the Army expert badge. You will be given several days in which you are able to qualify, if you should fail to qualify in those days the drill sergeants will try to get you additional chances to qualify but it is dependent on if the range is being used and if the company using it will allow you to try and qualify with them. If you are unable to hit at least 23 targets throughout white phase, you'll most likely be recycled to another company getting ready to start white phase to relearn marksmanship fundamentals.

Dress Blues

At some point during white phase or early in blue phase, you will be marched down to reception where you received your uniforms. Brining an empty duffle bag, you will be measured for your dress blue uniform. This will take a good part of the day and the entire day is usually set aside for this because every soldier in your company has to be measured for pants, shirts, hat size, jackets, gloves, shoes and an overcoat. You will also be given a lot of pins to pin onto your uniform at a later time. You will most likely be traveling back to the barracks in battle buddy teams although you could also be bussed back. When you get back do not put the pins on your uniform because you will be required to have them dry cleaned first. You can go ahead and remove the buttons because this will be asked of you before you send them off to the dry cleaners. The buttons can be removed but removing the coder pin from the back of the button. Be sure to put these someplace safe, if you have a zip lock bag I would put them inside of one of them and then place the bag into your shoebox.

Your beret is something you can work on though. For this you will be using a razor and shaving the fuzz off of your beret. Make sure you don't shave to hard though because this will cause you to put a hole in it. You should shave it until you see the lines of the fabric clearly (or simi clearly). I recommend on one of your trips to the PX grabbing yourself a bag of cheap razers because this will eat your razers up fast. There is also some cardboard inside of your beret, eventually you will be taking part of it out but until your drill sergeant instructs you on how he/she wants your beret to look you should leave it in. Your drill sergeant will show you how he wants it to look probably around blue phase and he/she will teach you how to mold it to your head. You will do this mostly in the last two weeks of basic training before your graduation ceremony. If you should happen to lose something or put a hole in your beret don't worry, your platoon will be given permission to run to send a few people over to the PX during the last couple weeks of training to pick up needed supplies. Someone will have a sheet of paper, they'll take your name down, what you want and how much money you gave them. (So, it's a good idea to run to the ATM when you have a chance and withdraw some money.) The platoon will also be picking up cleaning supplies and may ask for a donation if they decide to pick up some really good cleaning supplies before the final inspection.

Once you get your dress blues back from the cleaners you will then keep them in the plastic and put them away in your wall locker. You will have plenty of time to pin everything on before inspections and everyone will be helping everyone get the measurements right for where to pin everything. These measurements can be found in your blue book.

Blue Phase

Congratulations, you've passed your BRM and are looking forward the last bit of your training. Blue phase is by far the easiest and shortest of the three phases and you will know that there are very few obstacles left in your future at basic training.

Grenades

You're likely to spend at least half the day at the grenade range so expect MRE's for lunch or a portable lunch from the kitchen. The grenade course isn't that difficult to get through but you will be stressed because, you'll be handling grenades.

First, make sure you have your ear protection, eye protection, your Kevlar vest with both plates inside and your helmet. You'll start out be receiving a safety brief once you arrive at the range followed by a demonstration of different types of grenades. Pay close attention to the different types of grenades because you could be tested on this later. One safety tip I'm going to tell you right now is NEVER pull the safety pin until you are ready to throw the grenade. If you should pull it by mistake keep a firm grip on the grenade and call for a sergeant. They will tell you what to call out, it may be "Grenade" or some other phrase to let them know the emergency and they will come to you quickly and deal with the situation.

After the demonstrations are over you will be shown how to hold a grenade and you will be given a simulation grenade. You will then be taken down to another part of the range where you will be shown how to remove the safety clips on your grenade and properly throw it. For this, you will be standing in a line of about ten people side by side, and a sergeant will come by each of you in turn and tell you to throw your grenade. He will watch your every movement and tell you what you can improve on and then move to the next person. When you throw the grenade, they will be looking for height and distance, and the explosion isn't very loud from these, more like a pop. This goes really quick, and once every has thrown a grenade you will be sent out to retrieve the body of the grenade and the detonator, which you will bring back and sort into different containers before grabbing a new ready grenade simulator. You will then throw a couple of practice grenades before being moved to another section of the range.

At this next section, you will be given another lecture on safety and the procedure for throwing these next practice grenades. Here you will be going into these cement areas where a sergeant will be watching your every move and you will be graded. They will tell you to approach the area and before you enter you will say "Right hand, Right hand" to indicate you are throwing with your right hand. If you're a lefty you will say "Left hand, Left hand" and the sergeant will move to a position to better observe you. He will tell you to enter, and you will enter one leg at a time and get into the proper stance. He will then issue you commands to prep the grenade, strike a pose and throw. You are supposed to wait about 3 – 5 seconds after you throw before you hit the ground. The sergeant will then either give you a 'Go' or he/she will tell you what you did wrong and have you go to the back of the line and try again.

If for any reason you keep getting sent back to retry, try getting into a different sergeant's line to have them grade you. I failed three times from the same sergeant, who told me I was going down too quickly. After three times I was failed entirely and I had to come back during blue phase with a handful of others who had failed and tried again. When I came again I got the same sergeant who failed me 2 times in a row before I finally managed to get into a different sergeant's line for grading and he passed me right away.

Once you pass this section you will be sent to another part of the range far away from where you've been so far. This is where you will eventually be given a real live grenade. First, you'll stand in a line behind a large wall and you will be told where to stand in this line and how to squeeze together. Here you will be able to feel the shockwaves from the live grenades, even from behind a concrete wall. Once you get to the front of the line you will be told where you're going and you will be handed a grenade. You will quickly walk to the location you were told and you will do as you did before, tell the sergeant if you're left handed or right handed and then enter the area. There will be instructions over the loud speaker that are you to ignore. You will be taking all of your instructions from the sergeant, who will repeat the instructions when he is ready. He will give you the same commands you've been receiving for throwing a grenade, the only difference is that if you forget to go down or do something wrong, he may tackle you or take the grenade away and throw it to protect you from become injured. This rarely happens and I only heard of one or two people forgetting to go down because they wanted to see the explosion. Once you've finished throwing the grenade you will then leave the area and get lunch. Once everybody has finished throwing their grenades you will then head back to the barracks where you may go over the grenade types again.

If you should fail to properly throw a grenade, you may be given another chance to go with another company later on, but there is no guarantee of this because it will depend on scheduling and if another company will allow you to join them.

Buddy Team Live Fire

Buddy team live fire is where you will be using live ammo while running from objective to objective over a course. Before the course you will spend several days learning how to run the course and what commands you'll be calling out. For this course you will need your ear protection, eye protection, your Kevlar vest with both plates inside, your helmet and 3 magazines. Once you arrive on the course you'll receive instructions on how this is going to play out and you'll get your safety instructions just like every other course you've done before.

For this course you will start by walking doing a patrol when someone will call out "Fire, fire, fire!" and you will call out the number of enemies, the distance to the enemy and direction of the enemy. You will then be running for a given amount of time, stop, drop down to your stomach for 3 -5 seconds, stand back up and continue running to your first objective which will be a road barrier and you will fire at a target. You will also be giving commands while you're running. Once you and your buddy are at the first barrier one of you will give the proper command to let your battle buddy know you're getting ready to move. You will go through the proper steps for putting your weapon on safe, issuing the commands as you do so and then you will begin moving forward again. Once you get to a certain point or to the next barrier, whichever the drill sergeants have instructed you, you will give the proper command and provide cover fire while your battle buddy does the same thing you just did. You will do these two or three times, performing whatever the drill sergeants have instructed you to do, this may include low crawling, ranger crawl, dropping and running and even simulating throwing a grenade at the end.

You will be given a live demonstration of this just before you do it yourself and you may have to do these two or three times, the first time you may be doing this with blank rounds and your BFA will be on your weapon. The final time you do this though you will remove your BFA and you will be using live ammo. Because of this you will have to be extra careful in NOT flagging a battle buddy. If you flag a battle buddy your life is about to get a lot worse. A drill sergeant will be running next to you the entire time making sure you are in the right positions during the exercise. When you have live ammo you are expected, though not required, to hit the pop-up targets.

Once everyone is done, you'll likely have some ammo left over and drill sergeants hate to see extra ammo and so they will ask for weapons. If, and only if, you know your weapon will not jam up or have other problems should you offer your weapon up to one of the drill sergeants. They will then load the weapon and run the course firing the remaining rounds until they are all out. If your weapon doesn't jam up on them while they're doing everything they will be very pleased because they'll have fun firing the weapon, but if it's jamming they get frustrated and a frustrated drill sergeant can make you do extra work like having the platoon low crawl back to their assault bags from the range. Also, if a weapon is jamming on them because it's dirty, they're going to be much harder on you when it comes time for cleaning your weapon. Please keep in mind that the commands and procedure was the one I was given when I went though my training but the procedure and commands could be different for you.

NIC at Night

Night Infiltration Course (NIC at Night) is where you will be doing the low crawl with your rifle over 50 yards at night while having live ammunition fired above your heads using tracer rounds and flares.

First, you'll need your Kevlar vest, helmet, ear pro, eye pro, rifle and if you're lucky, your knee and elbow pads in your uniform. You will start off by lining up in formations and someone will come around and inspect you to ensure you are ready for this. You will be lead down range where you will line up behind a wall. When you are given the go ahead, a timer will start and you will pull yourself up and over the wall and start low crawling as quickly as you can to the other end. There will be fenced off areas you may have to go around and be careful around these areas because this is where simulated explosions will go off. From time to time a flare will be shot up into the air, when this happens you are to freeze, close your eyes and keep your head down. You'll want your eyes closed just enough to block out a majority of the light caused by the flare so as not to ruin your night vision, but you'll want to be able to tell when the flare dies as well so that when it's out you can continue. There may be between 2 – 5 flares fired up into the air, this is a good time to relax and take a breather, each flare lasted around 20 – 30 seconds when I did this. Once you reach the other end of the field a sergeant will tell you that you can stand up and get behind a given area. You will all then be escorted back up to where you originally formed up.

While this sounds like a quick event to do, it actually takes quite a while because they break you down into groups. Remember, under no circumstance should you ever raise from the front crawl while on this field, if you do you risk being shot. The bullets flying above are real and although they are flying well above you where there's little risk of you getting hit even in the kneeling position, you do not want to risk your life and that's exactly what you will be doing because if a bullet doesn't find you a drill sergeant will and they can recycle you for doing something stupid like that.

Battle Team Tactics

With battle team tactics you and a battle buddy will be working together to move from one covered position to the next. You will start off walking in a patrol style walk when someone will call out "Contact" or "Enemy fire" at which point both you and your battle buddy will call out something along the lines of: "Contact, Contact, Contact, five enemies, two hundred yards North." While running to your first covered position. Once you and your battle buddy have taken up the correct stance you and your battle buddy must coordinate moving to the next covered position. If you're moving first you will call out something along the lines of: "Cover me while I move!" and your battle buddy will reply: "I've got you covered!" At this point your battle buddy will be providing cover fire for you, you will place your weapon on safe, bring the barrel safely down and begin making your way to the next position.

The obstacle and procedures your drill sergeants will have you follow will be explained in detail, but you can expect to do a low crawl, high crawl, run and drop down for five seconds and maybe something special if the drill sergeants want you to simulate throwing a grenade.

Once you've reached your next covered firing position you will call out to your battle buddy: "Set" and it will now be your battle buddy's turn to move. These same commands will be used until you get to your final position where you may be required to call out "LOA" which stand for Limit Of Advance. This will be the final cover you will take and at which point you may or may not have a new command set for throwing a grenade.

You will rehearse this several times either at the barracks, out in the P.T. field or where ever your drill sergeants find useful to do some trial runs and get you use to calling out the commands and doing the actions they want you to do. Once you've practiced enough times you will eventually be taken out to a course where a larger version will be set up and you will do a couple of runs with blank firing rounds on your weapon that you will fire off while providing covering fire.

Once you have done this once or twice, you may be giving live rounds with pop up targets that you will fire upon. It is very important to remember to maintain full control of your weapon at all times. A drill sergeant will not hesitate to throw you down if you flag one of your battle buddies or are demonstrating unsafe weapon handling.

Machine Gun

Who doesn't want to fire off a machine gun? If you have no desire to fire one then that's just too bad because you're going to be firing one! You will probably get to march down to this range where you will be introduced to a machine gun. I fired the 240 and the 249, although when you get your chance to go through they may have newer machine guns so I won't be going into any of the details about how to fire them. I can tell you that you will be broken down into groups and you will then be given a class on how to approach the weapon, how to load it, how to fire it, how to check it in the event of a jam and how to switch the barrels out. Once your class is over you will put on all the necessary gear and collect your belt of ammo. This is a little more relaxed then when you were at the range firing your rifle and there will be an instructor at each weapon. When it's your turn to fire the instructors are very laid back assuming you aren't an idiot and try to do something very stupid. You will fire off around 100 or 200 rounds of ammo and then you will leave.

Once everyone is done firing you will do a police call and collect all the ammo casings and link casings separating the two into different containers and picking up any trash in the area.

Other Weapons

You will have some brief exposure to several other weapons while you're in training and you may even get to fire some training rounds. One of the weapons we got to fire was the AT-4 rocket launcher. We fired tracer rounds out of this weapon and the person who had achieved the best score in weapons qualification was allowed to fire a live round at a tank that was used as target practice. Another weapon we got to fire dummy rounds out of was the M-320 grenade launcher. You will be instructed on all the safety procedures for handling each of these weapons before you're even allowed to pick them up. After you have demonstrated your competency in handling them you will be lined up and allowed to fire the dummy rounds.

16K Ruck March

Your 16K Ruck March is typically one of the last things that you will do requirement wise in basic training. It should go without saying that this is going to be the longest, hardest ruck you've done. In the warmer months you will start out early in the morning (or very late at night before your usual bedtime) so that you won't be getting beat down so badly by the sun and thus preventing you from overheating during the day too. During the colder months you may still start out earlier in the morning but you may see the sun still, or you'll start out before it gets dark out so you're still mostly out of the sun. The ruck march may have a special ending at some point called something like victory hill where you will go through a special ceremony of completion. (Just to be safe, pack your beret in your ruck.)

For my first cycle, my company did an 8K ruck one way, and then an 8K ruck back, and upon returning, there were little fireworks going off, music playing, refreshments and even the battalion commander was there waiting to congratulate everyone, and then everyone got to sleep for about ten hours. During my second cycle, we did our ruck march up to the Nick at Night course, killed a number of hours, did the NIC at Night course and then took a bus back to the barracks where we still received the fireworks and some congratulations followed by going to bed.

Final Inspection

Now comes the most stressful part of your training, the final inspection. From the moment your 16K ruck march is done until the final inspection is completed you will be constantly stressed out. First, you will have to clean all of your equipment, everything you were ever issued has to be in a 'like new' state. You will be taking everything apart, cleaning it, and then putting it back together and the way we found that worked best was to have one group of people take apart the ruck sacks and clean them, dry them and put them back together and get them back to everyone, have one group of people take the shower curtains outside and scrub them good, dry them and bring them back in. Everything will have to be cleaned. You will pull up all of the tape on the floor, clean the floor to look amazing, perhaps you'll scrub it down by hand, move the lockers and clean behind and under them, clean your weapons to be spotless etc.

Basically, picture the most, obscene stereotyped inspection from a military father checking his sons room, or something along those lines and picture that being lenient. During the final inspection, the battalion commander will be coming to each barracks, quizzing random people, checking how clean everything is and since this is a streamer event and more importantly, because the battalion commander is there, the drill sergeants from other platoons will be checking air vents, around fire extinguishers and everything they possibly can to discredit another platoon in order to make their own look better.

The lockers must all look identical and what will happen is one person's locker will be selected out of the four platoons to work as the demo locker and everyone has to make sure their locker is precisely the same. (You will be able to store additional items in your duffle bag that is not on display.) So, if the demo locker has their socks folded a certain way and there are 3 pairs of black socks, 3 pairs of white socks and five pairs of green socks, then you will need to have the same number of socks in the same order and folded the same way. If for any reason you don't have enough pairs of socks, you'll either be buying some or borrowing a pair for inspection purposes.

You will spend about a solid week doing nothing but cleaning in order to get ready for this inspection and you will have people working around the clock on this. If you have a few people that are really good at cleaning weapons, have them check and clean everybody's weapon. This is also the time a few people from each platoon will be allowed to go to the PX for supplies and depending on how badly your platoon wants to win this award you may be buying additional and better cleaning supplies. This is also a good time to buy additional berets or gear you may be needing. When we were within two days of the inspection, we roped off all but two bathroom stalls and two showers for use so that we would only have to clean 2 of them right before inspection. New tape was put down for the kill lines. The beds were not even slept in, we would sleep on the floor because a lot of your equipment has to be laid out on your bed in a specific order and each display must look identical and to make sure every one of them was in order, we would take a cord, tie it from one bed and go to the end of another bed, make sure every bed was lined up perfectly, spaced evenly apart and then we would take that same line and run it over the equipment from one end to the other making sure that everything lined up. Your dress blue uniforms will also be inspected and so every little detail on them has to be perfect. Try to keep your dress blues in the cleaning bag once you've positioned all of the badges and medals. The drill sergeants would come by now and then to help tell us where to clean that they would be inspecting and would get flashlights and perform inspections of our weapons. During the inspection, your rifle will be completely disassembled on a towel in front of you and you may be chosen to put your rifle together and you will be timed.

During my first cycle, about three days before the inspection we had a drill sergeant come in while we were cleaning and listening to music (because we were given a radio to listen to while cleaning) and he wanted to speak with us and told us to turn the radio down. Sadly, the private that went to turn it down was moving too slowly and couldn't seem to turn it down right away and the drill sergeant went ballistic pulling the radio cord out of the wall and smashing it on the ground, he then had everyone toe the line and smoked everyone for a good thirty minutes lecturing us on how we'd become complacent and that we were still in training and we should always move with a purpose. While he was right about us becoming complacent, the whole thing was also staged. Because I was injured I was assigned to be a weapons guard with another injured battle buddy while everyone else went to eat chow, (They would bring weapons guards food in a to go tray.) I could hear them laughing and joking about what had just happened.

With my second cycle, I remember two nights before the inspection the senior drill sergeant came in, did a quick inspection and told us how disappointed he was in us, throwing stuff around saying how dirty it was and just walking out of the bay while one of our other drill sergeants came up and told us that he had never seen him so upset before. (This was an act and they do it every cycle and they even told us as much after we won) They want you to work for this award harder than any other award, it means a lot to them. In both cycles, the night before the inspection nobody slept, we all cleaned and made sure everything was perfect.

Final Days

Once the final inspection is complete you will be in your final days before you graduate and all of the hard stuff is over. Now you'll be spending your remaining days returning the equipment you were issued (the stuff you signed for once you arrived at the barracks) and you will be practicing for the final ceremonies. You will also be reviewing your records, new orders and getting any additional shots you may need.

You will undergo two ceremonies, one will be on family day, where you will be presented before your family and they will be told of what you have accomplished. After the ceremony is completed you will be released to your family to go anywhere you want (as long as you don't leave a certain area) but you'll be able to go out to eat, see the sights, go to a hotel or anything along those lines. If you don't have family coming you can ask if you can go with a battle buddy and his family. Sometimes two battle buddies without family will be allowed to battle each other to the PX to buy some snacks and wonder around with a pass signed by the drill sergeant. You will have a curfew and must be back by a certain time or you risk losing spending the day with your family on graduation day.

Graduation day will hold a lot of ceremony, several people will be chosen to wear special gear and parade it during the ceremony. I won't go into much detail about this because the several that I was able to witness were all different but were very well rehearsed. Again, you will be released to your family once it's over and have a curfew. Don't do anything stupid while you're out because you are still in uniform and you can still be given orders, but more importantly you are representing the United States Army and your actions reflect on them. I have heard of people doing a stupid prank or something else stupid where they were recycled to day one of basic training because they thought it would be funny to do something.

On your last day at basic training you will either be put on a bus to go to AIT or you will be released to someone who will drive you in their personally owned vehicle (POV).

MISC Things to Know

Army Physical Fitness Test: You will take at a minimum of 3 APFT, one in each phase of your training. The test is divided into three parts; <u>Push-ups</u>, <u>Sit-ups</u> and <u>Running</u>. A demonstration of how to correctly perform a proper push-up and sit-up will shown prior to your testing. You will be instructed on how the test will be carried out just before the test as well. You will have two minutes to do as many push-ups or sit-ups as you can. A drill sergeant will be counting how many you have done and they should be counting the number of correct ones you have done, if they keep repeating a number then you are doing something wrong. Once the push-ups are done and then the sit-ups, you will be taken to either a track or a stretch of road that has been blocked off for your two-mile run.

It is really important to be able to always pass your APFT however, if you should have trouble during the first two in basic training this just means you need to work harder with your exercising. Your third and what should be your final APFT at basic training is the most important one though because this is for your record, this one determines if you graduate from basic training. You must pass every event in the APFT by achieving the minimum score to get a passing score, failing by one second or one push-up will fail you in the entire APFT. Additionally, there is a maximum you can really to get 100 points for that particular event. If you should go over the maximum that's great but you can not get better than 100 points per even giving you a total of 300 for a perfect APFT. There is one exception to this rule though and that is if you can go beyond the limit in every event, then they will calculate your score in a way that allows for a score of over 300. If you would like to see what you need in order to pass go to the website: https://www.goarmy.com/soldier-life/fitness-and-nutrition/exercise.html

Sick Call: If you should become sick / injured you will need to go to sick call. Before you go to sleep you will fill out a sheet located at the fireguard station saying that you are going to sick call and what for. These sheets are then collected and are collected by fireguard and taken to the drill sergeant in charge of C.Q. for the night. The next morning you will wake up earlier than the others (You will be told what time you have to be in formation and what uniform to wear) ensure you have your CAC and you will assemble in a designated area. A drill sergeant or the training sergeant will then come out and do a roll call while handing you back your sheet of paper you filled out and an MRE. You must also have a battle buddy, typically someone from your platoon is best and it must be someone of the same sex (opposite sexes will never be allowed to battle buddy anywhere). You must go and return from sick call together. You will then be either shuttled over to sick call or told to march yourselves down to sick call. Once you arrive at sick call you will eat your MRE and wait for them to open. They will divide you into groups and they will take certain groups first. You will wait in line with your paperwork and your CAC, both of which is checked at the door before you can go in. If you forgot your CAC you will either have to get a battle buddy to go back with you for it or call your company to pick you up with a battle buddy, get your CAC and return. (You can imagine how unhappy that will make everyone.)

You will probably be given a mask to put over your face so that you don't get other people sick (or pick something up yourself), you will check in with someone at a counter, then have your tempter and pulse taken. After this you will be told to take a seat and you will form a line via your seats and wait to be called or for the line to just move up. You can spend up to half a day at sick call easily because of all the people there. If a problem is beyond their ability to diagnose they can send you to a hospital for things such as an MRI or surgery if it's needed.

If you're sick, they'll probably issue you some Ibuprofen and send you on your way with paperwork showing the medicine they issued you. If you're injured and have something like stress fractures or a sprain or broken bones, then they'll put you on profile limiting what you can do while in training and give you Ibuprofen. If you receive a profile, you may be required to report back to sick call after a given amount of time to see if you've recovered enough to be taken off of profile, or the profile may simply expire after a given amount of time. While on profile you will be required to keep a copy of the profile on you at all times. You will need to make a copy of your profile and give one to your drill sergeant, one to the training sergeant (if they request it) and then one for yourself. If the profile expires or you are taken off profile always keep a copy of that profile for your records later on. If you return to sick call to be taken off profile you will receive a profile with R.T.D. written on it which stands for Return To Duty. If the injury was serious enough, you may be given an L.O.D. which stands for Line Of Duty. These are more serious and if you receive to many (I was told three) you will be discharged.

Keep in mind, it's always best to be honest when the doctors/ nurses ask you a question, but there are times you will want to be careful about what you say. An example of this is, once I had my surgery I was taken back to the barracks and the next day I had to go to sick call for a checkup. They asked me some routine questions, how I was feeling, was there any pain and then they asked me what color my urine was. Without thinking I answered yellow to that last question and the doctor looked over to the nurse and said told her to get an IV in me so they could hydrate me. The correct answer to that last question should've been 'Clear' and I would've been spared one of several needles I got that day.

Dental: Is done in the same manner as sick call, just held at a different place. The Army doesn't really want you going to dental in basic training unless it's an emergency or something that must be taken care of. They would rather you wait until you get to AIT because they only have you for 10 weeks and that's not a lot of time to learn everything they need to teach you.

Heat Casualty: A heat casualty is someone that has over heated and typically loses consciousnesses. When this happens, a soldier will have his/ her jacket stripped off and sometimes pants as well and then they will be covered completely in sheets have soaking in ice water in order to bring the body temperature down. One way to prevent becoming a heat cat is to stay hydrated.

Heat Cat 1 – 5: There are different levels of heat categories and depending on the type of training you are doing and more importantly the heat outside, a drill sergeant may call out a heat category level such as 'heat cat 3'. This tells the soldiers how their uniform is expected to look, usually the sleeves may be slightly rolled up along with your pant legs being rolled up a little to better disperse the heat. Drill sergeants will go over this with you and will even demonstrate it the first time it's called. If the heat is excessive or if the drill sergeants think its better for the trainees, they will have stations everyone will go though and usually submerge their arms in ice water for about thirty seconds.

Hydration: Dehydration will drop more soldiers than any thing else during your time in training. Make sure to drink plenty of water and a way you can tell if you're drinking enough water is by the color of your urine. There will probably be charts around your latrine and various other places showing you what the different colors of urine mean. The important color is clear. If your urine is clear then you're drinking enough water. If it's a bright yellow you should drink some more water. Generally speaking, the darker the color, the more water you should be drinking.

You'll hear the drill sergeants constantly yelling 'Drink water'. They must think it fixes all problems because if you have a cramp and tell them about it, they will tell you to drink water. If you get sick, drink water, if you break a bone... they may tell you to go to sick call in the morning but until then... drink water.

Lectures

From time to time you'll be taken to a classroom where you will be lectured on various subjects ranging from weapon safety to Land Navigation all the way to S.H.A.R.P. training. Bring a notebook and two pens (one for a battle buddy that forgot theirs) and get ready for a long class. These are some of the most trying times in basic training, trying to stay awake during class. If you find yourself struggling to stay awake, some drill sergeants will allow you to move to the side or the back of the classroom and stand up. Others will let you fall asleep and then punish you by having you do push-ups or the squat bender (or some other exercise) during class until they think you can stay awake (though even that doesn't help). If you can't stay awake, write something down in your notes, write the soldiers creed, anything (that won't get you in trouble if a drill sergeant reads it, so no letters) to get you focused. You should be paying attention to the speaker, but after a few hour-long briefs about S.H.A.R.P. I know it can get hard to stay awake. This would also be a good time to try and study something like the P.T. drills.

I found that drinking water helped me stay awake (but also needed to really use the latrine when it was all over). You will need to find a way to stay awake or learn to sleep with your eyes open because drill sergeants will be actively looking for people sleeping or dozing off.

Church Services

Church services are held on Sundays, you will be instructed to sign up for services the day before and you will be expected to attend if you sign up. There are several different types of services offered at different times so make sure you sign up for the correct service and do not sign up for multiple services unless you're instructed that you can do so. At my basic training, the Jewish service even got bagels to eat so if for no other reason you can go for the food.

Chaplain

A chaplain will be available for you to speak with if you should ever need any guidance ranging from depression, personal matters going on at home, spiritual problems and even SHARP related issues. They will keep things confidential unless you ask them to take an issue public. The chaplain will let you know how he or she can be contacted while you are in training. Do not think of yourself as week if you need to seek one out, being able to speak with a chaplain may give you the strength to get through it.

S.H.A.R.P

Sexual Harassment Assault Response & Prevention is talked about a lot during your time in training. This training will cover what S.H.A.R.P. is, how to avoid violating it and what the punishment for violating it is. If you would like to get a good general idea about S.H.A.R.P. you can google "Tea consent" and you can watch an entertaining video that covers the basics. I don't want to down play how important this subject matter is because it is important, but you will be getting so many S.H.A.R.P. briefings that just hearing the words 'S.H.A.R.P.' will cause you to grown but violating S.H.A.R.P. is very easy and you could find yourself in violation when you thought you were just having innocent fun with a battle buddy. Pay attention and if you have to question yourself if it could be considered S.H.A.R.P. then it's best to avoid doing it.

While on this subject, remember that you're here to train, not to find your soul mate. It's alright to make good friends and all of that while you're in training but don't try to start a relationship here. You don't need the distraction and you definitely don't want to violate S.H.A.R.P. in any way.

ACH	Army Combat Helmet
AGR	Ability Group Run
A.I.T.	Advanced Individual Training
A.P.F.T.	Army Physical Fitness Test
AR	Army Regulation
BCT	Basic Combat Training
BFA	Blank Firing Adapter
BMC	Basic Military Communications
BRM	Basic Rifle Marksmanship
CAC	Common Access Card
CBRN	Chemical, Biological, Radiological and Nuclear
CQ	Charge of Quarters
DEERS	Defense Enrollment Eligibility Reporting System
EO	Equal Opportunity
FM	Field Manual
FTX	Field Training Exercise
IED	Improvised Explosive device
IFAK	Improved First Aid Kit

JAG	Judge Advocate General
LES	Leave and Earnings Statement
LOA	Limit of Advance
LOD	Line of Duty
MEPS	Military Entrance Processing Station
MOS	Military Occupation Specialty
PC	Protective Cover / Patrol Cap
PNN	Private News Network (Gossip around base)
POV	Personally Owned Vehicle
PT	Physical Training
PX	Postal Exchange
RTD	Return To Duty
S.H.A.R.P.	Sexual Harassment Assault Response & Prevention
SOP	Standard Operating Procedure
S.P.O.R.T.S.	Slap, Pull, Observe, Release, Tap, Squeeze
TC3	Tactical Combat Casualty Care
UCMJ	Uniform Code of Military Justice

Phonetic Alphabet

A – Alpha

B – Bravo

C - Charlie

D - Delta

E - Echo

F - Foxtrot

G - Golf

H – Hotel

I – India

J - Juliet

K – Kilo

L - Lima

M – Mike

N - November

O – Oscar

P - Papa

Q - Quebec

R - Romeo

S - Sierra

T - Tango

U - Uniform

V – Victor

W - Whiskey

X - X-ray

Y - Yankee

Z - Zulu

Morse Code

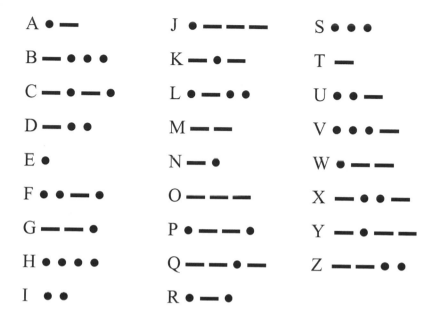

A ● — J ● — — — S ● ● ●

B — ● ● ● K — ● — T —

C — ● — ● L ● — ● ● U ● ● —

D — ● ● M — — V ● ● ● —

E ● N — ● W ● — —

F ● ● — ● O — — — X — ● ● —

G — — ● P ● — — ● Y — ● — —

H ● ● ● ● Q — — ● — Z — — ● ●

I ● ● R ● — ●

You won't need to know Morse code in basic training and I only added it because sometimes people get bored and just want to learn something new, especially people that are injured and waiting to heal up before starting their training again.

Cadence

Starting in white phase (usually) you'll be introduced to Cadences, which are songs you'll sing while marching and help you keep in step. I've listed a few that were favorites in my companies and will help you to know if you're ever called upon to lead the cadence.

They say that in the Army

Leader: They say that in the Army the chicken is mighty fine

Everyone: Who says that? They say that in the Army the chicken is mighty fine, one jumped off the table and started marking time.

Oh Lord I wanna go

But they won't let me go home.

Leader: They say that in the Army the coffee is mighty fine

Everyone: Who says that? They say that in the Army the coffee is mighty fine. It looks like muddy water and tastes like turpentine.

Leader: They say that in the Army the biscuits are mighty fine

Everyone: Who says that? They say that in the Army the biscuits are mighty fine. One rolled off a table and killed a friend of mine

Leader: They say that in the Army the pancakes are mighty fine

Everyone: Who says that? They say that in the Army the pancakes are mighty fine. You can try to chew them, but you're only wasting time.

Leader: They say that in the Army the money is mighty fine

Everyone: Who says that? They say that in the Army the money is mighty fine. They pay you one hundred dollars and take back ninety-nine.

Airborne Rangers

Walking down the street one day

I met a total stranger

He asked me what I wanna be

I told him Airborne Ranger

Airboooooorn (Lock and Load, pull the trigger, Shoot that son of a...),

RANGEEEEEEERS (die die why won't you die!) LEAD THE WAY

My buddies in a foxhole... A bullet in his head... The medic says he's wounded... But I know that he's dead

Airboooooorn (Lock and Load, pull the trigger, Shoot that son of a...),

RANGEEEEEEERS (die die why won't you die!) LEAD THE WAY

I'm sitting in my foxhole

Sharpening my knife

When out jump the enemy

I had to end his life

Airbooooooorn (Lock and Load, pull the trigger, Shoot that son of a…),

RANGEEEEEEERS (die die why won't you die!) LEAD THE WAY

There's choppers flying overhead

Come to get the wounded! Come to get the dead

Airbooooooorn (Lock and Load, pull the trigger, Shoot that son of a…),

RANGEEEEEEERS (die die why won't you die!) LEAD THE WAY

Momma Can't You See (While running)

Mama mama can't you see,
what the army's done to me.

They put me in a barber's chair,
spun me around I had no hair.

Mama mama can't you see,
what the army's done to me.

They took away my favorite jeans,
now I'm wearing Army greens.

Mama mama can't you see,
what the army's done to me.

I use to date a beauty queen,
now I date my M16.

End Notes

Basic training may feel like it's going to last forever, but it does get easier the further in you get and the more use to things you become. If you start getting overwhelmed ask your battle buddies for help. If you see someone struggling with something, go up to them and offer them help, sometimes all someone may need is someone to talk to and a little encouragement. I saw several soldiers on the verge of quitting but because someone was willing to listen and encourage them, they were able to push through and come out on top. You will form friendships that you will always treasure with your battle buddies and you will accomplish things you never dreamed yourself doing before. When you're finished you will be filled with a sense of pride the day you graduate from basic training.

I would love to be able to tell you that things only get easier after this training but I don't know where you're headed. For me it did get easier. A.I.T. was much more laid back than basic training was, and once I finished that and got to my unit things became easier still and even more laid back. It's still very important to always remember your military baring, respecting officers and NCO's by addressing them properly and standing at the correct position, but I'm sure you'll find your military experience completely different than that of basic training. If you're interested in learning some more about the army I recommend you go to https://www.goarmy.com/ This site has a lot of good information about the army including different MOS's to look at and different ways you can join the army. This website also has a search feature and you can find nearly everything you would like to know.

I would like to close by thanking those of you, no matter what branch of the service you choose to serve in, for your service. We are the greatest country in the world and it's because of the men and women like you who serve, that we can keep this country safe.